The Intellectual's
CHECKLIST

The Intellectual's
CHECKLIST

ART
ARCHITECTURE
HISTORY
PHILOSOPHY
SCIENCE & TECHNOLOGY
LITERATURE
MATHEMATICS
MUSIC
POLITICS

More Than **350** Esoteric Facts, Figures, and Philosophies Only the Smartest People Know

Richard J. Wallace
& James V. Wallace

Adamsmedia
Avon, Massachusetts

Published by
Adams Media, a division of F+W Media, Inc.
57 Littlefield Street, Avon, MA 02322. U.S.A.
www.adamsmedia.com

ISBN 10: 1-4405-3028-9
ISBN 13: 978-1-4405-3028-9
eISBN 10: 1-4405-3114-5
eISBN 13: 978-1-4405-3114-9

Printed in the United States of America.

10   9   8   7   6   5   4   3   2   1

Library of Congress Cataloging-in-Publication Data
is available from the publisher.

This publication is designed to provide accurate and authoritative information
with regard to the subject matter covered. It is sold with the understanding that
the publisher is not engaged in rendering legal, accounting, or other professional
advice. If legal advice or other expert assistance is required, the services of a
competent professional person should be sought.
— From a *Declaration of Principles* jointly adopted by a Committee of the
American Bar Association and a Committee of Publishers and Associations

Many of the designations used by manufacturers and sellers to distinguish their
product are claimed as trademarks. Where those designations appear in this
book and Adams Media was aware of a trademark claim, the designations have
been printed with initial capital letters.

This book is available at quantity discounts for bulk purchases.
For information, please call 1-800-289-0963.

Contents

Introduction

All five movements of Beethoven's Missa solemnis. Check.
The films that Kurosawa based on Western works. Check.
Dante's Nine Circles of Hell. Check.

These are the sorts of elegant erudition every self-respecting intellectual should know—inside and out. In *The Intellectual's Checklist*, aspiring pundits, poets, and philosophers will find the arcane checklists that reveal whether they are truly well-versed enough in the arts and sciences of the obscure to warrant the esteemed moniker *intellectual*.

From Nietzsche to Newton, Einstein to Eisenstadt, Sappho to Sartre, this elucidating volume gives you all the esoterica you need to bask in the knowledge that you really do know everything. (Or at least you will once you've read this book.)

You may have worked hard to earn a degree—or devote persistent efforts to the pursuit of intellectual interests—and feel justifiably proud of your attainments. *The Intellectual's Checklist* is designed to help you celebrate, by way of demonstrating your intellect to yourself and others.

The goal of *The Intellectual's Checklist* is to present information in checklist format that every self-respecting intellectual should know. In the following pages you will find information about important events and the people involved in them, creative accomplishments, influential successes, and disastrous failures.

Topics covered in this book include architecture, art, history, literature, mathematics, music, nature, philosophy, politics, science, and technology. Within each topic, facts and ideas have been chosen and placed in lists. You have an opportunity to compare your understanding of a subject—whether a person, place, event, object, or concept—against these checklists. You may be asked how many of the buildings designed by Frank Lloyd Wright you have seen in person. You may be requested to match early American artists with their works. Or you may need to recall your knowledge of scientific or mathematical principles. Each checklist will test your knowledge or perception in its own way or from a particular perspective. But specialized knowledge is not required to enjoy this book. You won't need an advanced degree in any single area, although you will need an above-average knowledge of a broad range of subjects. Each checklist will give you a new opportunity to confirm your status as an intellectual.

As you read through each checklist, give yourself one point for correctly identifying all the elements or for correctly answering the question posed. Note your total in the box at the end of the checklist. For each two-page spread, there's a bigger box for you to add up the answers to the three checklists in that spread. At the end of each chapter, you can add up all of your correct answers for that chapter and turn to the answer key section, where you'll have the opportunity to rate how intellectual you are on the subject. Finally, at the end of the book, you'll have a chance to add up how you did for all six chapters and learn the truth. Are you a real intellectual, or just a wannabe?

Enjoy!

Chapter 1

Art and Architecture

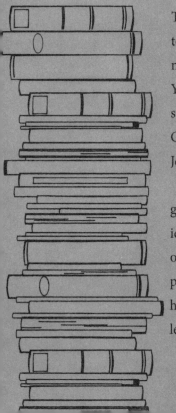

The checklists in the Art and Architecture chapter cover graphic arts and motion pictures as well as architecture. You'll have the opportunity to demonstrate your knowledge of topics such as Greek contributions to art and Thomas Jefferson's influence on architecture.

As you read through the checklists, give yourself one point for correctly identifying all the elements in a checklist or for correctly answering the question posed. At the end of the chapter, you'll have the opportunity to rate how intellectual you are on these subjects.

DIFFERENT STROKES

Which of these artists' works have you seen?

* Pablo Picasso
* Salvador Dali
* Claude Monet
* Vincent van Gogh
* Édouard Manet
* Andy Warhol
* Jackson Pollock
* Michelangelo
* Rembrandt van Rijn

POINTS

ART FOR ART'S SAKE

How many of these museums have you visited in person?

* Musée du Louvre, Paris
* British Museum, London
* Metropolitan Museum of Art, New York City
* National Gallery of Art, Washington, D.C.
* The Hermitage, Saint Petersburg
* Museo del Prado, Madrid

POINTS

HAND ME THAT BRUSH, GROK

Can you answer these questions about the earliest examples of human art?

1. The caves in Lascaux, France, contain prehistoric paintings of about how many figures?
2. The Atamira Cave in Spain contains some art that may be up to how many years old?
3. The Chauvet-Pont-d'Arc Cave in southern France contains hundreds of paintings of what?
4. The oldest undisputed example of prehistoric art is how many years old?
5. What is this item of prehistoric art called, and where is it located?

ANSWER:
1. 600
2. 18, 500
3. Animals
4. 35,000–40,000
5. It is the Venus of Hohle Fels figurine from Schelklingen, Germany

POINTS

COMBINED POINTS

BUILDING THE BEST

How many of the buildings of these Pritzker Prize winners can you name?

1. Eduardo Souto de Moura (Portugal) designed _____ in Braga, Portugal
2. Kazuyo Sejima and Ryue Nishizawa (Japan) designed _____ in Toledo, Ohio
3. Peter Zumthor (Switzerland) designed _____ in Vals, Switzerland
4. Jean Nouvel (France) designed _____ in Paris
5. Richard Rogers (England) designed _____ in Paris

ANSWER:

1. The Municipal Stadium
2. The Toledo Museum of Art's Glass Pavilion
3. The Thermal Baths
4. The Arab World Institute
5. The Centre Pompidou

POINTS

TIME AND GREEK ART MARCHES ON

Greek art was well developed by the fifth century B.C. How many of these facts about Greek art of that period do you know?

* Many Greek vase painters had taken up wall painting with tempera
* These more expressive decorative arts included murals and works on wood panels
* Some artists created paintings on parchment
* None of the murals from this time survive
* Historical documents tell us that Parrhasius used spatial perspective to create depth
* Zeuxis painted such realistic grapes that birds tried to eat them

POINTS

GETTING IT WRIGHT

How many of these buildings designed by Frank Lloyd Wright have you seen?

* Taliesin, Spring Green, Wisconsin
* Taliesin West, Scottsdale, Arizona
* Solomon R. Guggenheim Museum, New York City
* Child of the Sun, Florida Southern College, Lakeland, Florida
* Marin County Civic Center, San Rafael, California

POINTS

COMBINED POINTS

GRAND HOTELS

Which of the following hotels selected by the National Trust for Historic Preservation have you seen?

* Fairmont Hotel San Francisco
* Grand Hotel, Mackinac Island, Michigan
* InterContinental Chicago Magnificent Mile
* Mohonk Mountain House, New Paltz, New York
* Omni Bedford Springs Resort, Bedford, Pennsylvania
* Wentworth Mansion, Charleston, South Carolina

POINTS

HUMBLE BEGINNINGS

The art of the motion picture dates to the late nineteenth century. Which of the following facts did you know about its origins?

* Americans, French, British, and German inventors worked on the development of motion pictures
* Credit is given to Thomas Edison's lab for development of the Kinetoscope in 1889
* The Kinetoscope was not a projector; a person looked through a peephole to view the film
* Edison's team also developed the Kinetograph, a motion picture camera

POINTS

JUST A TOY

Which of these statements about early motion pictures are true?

1. Edison did not bother to obtain an international patent for the Kinetoscope
2. The French Lumière brothers made their own version of the motion picture camera
3. In 1925, the first public showing of a projected motion picture took place in Paris
4. Watching a movie through a peephole was more popular than projection because people enjoyed the individual, personal experience

ANSWER: Statements 1 and 2 are true; statements 3 and 4 are false.

POINTS

COMBINED POINTS

A FRENCH INNOVATOR

Some individuals saw the commercial opportunities from new motion picture technology. Were you aware of the following?

* Georges Méliès was among those who saw the first motion picture shown in Paris
* He acquired a camera and built his own studio near Paris to make movies
* Méliès wrote his own scripts, designed sets, and hired actors
* From 1899 to 1912, Méliès made more than 400 films
* *A Trip to the Moon* (*Le voyage dans la Lune*), made in 1902, is his most famous film

POINTS

STYLIN'

Match the following structures with their architectural style.

A. Marcel Breuer-designed house, Baltimore, Maryland
B. Seagram Building, New York City
C. Capitol Building, Washington, D.C.
D. Tribune Tower, Chicago, Illinois
E. Mercer House, Savannah, Georgia
F. Hoover Dam, Boulder City, Nevada

1. Greek Revival
2. Bauhaus
3. Italianate
4. Art Deco
5. International style
6. Gothic Revival

ANSWER: A, 2; B, 5; C, 1; D, 6; E, 3; F, 4

POINTS

OF PAINT AND PYRAMIDS

Can you identify which of these statements about ancient Egyptian art are true?

1. A uniform style of art was used in Egypt for about 500 years
2. Artists were encouraged to create highly individual works of art
3. Egyptian artists developed a highly conventional way of depicting human figures, with the figure's head and legs in profile and the torso facing forward
4. Alexander the Great's invasion in 331 B.C. brought Greek influences to Egyptian art

ANSWER:
1. False. This uniform style of art was used for more than 2,000 years.
2. False. Artists were highly trained and specialized to maintain consistency.
3. True.
4. True.

POINTS

COMBINED POINTS

THE FED

Federal-style architecture was a strong influence in early American buildings and was popular between 1780 and 1830. How many Federal buildings are you familiar with?

* State House, Boston, Massachusetts
* Davenport House, Savannah, Georgia
* Holladay House, Orange, Virginia
* Julia Row, New Orleans, Louisiana
* Old Derby Academy, Hingham, Massachusetts

POINTS

GREEKS GO ARTISTIC

Museums worldwide contain examples of impressive Greek art. Were you aware that:

* By 700 B.C., Greek painters used a black glaze to create narrative scenes on vases
* Many vases depict battle scenes and mythological characters
* Later examples of vases show real-life events
* The paintings used some conventions for details, but were more natural than earlier styles
* Egyptian vase painters' individual efforts started the tradition of independent artistic style

POINTS

AMERICA'S FIRST ARCHITECT

Charles Bulfinch (1763–1844) is considered the first native-born American professional architect. How many of his buildings can you name?

1. _____
2. _____
3. _____
4. _____
5. _____

ANSWER:

* Massachusetts General Hospital, Boston, Massachusetts
* Maine State House, Augusta, Maine
* University Hall, Harvard University, Cambridge, Massachusetts
* Faneuil Hall expansion, Boston, Massachusetts
* Old State House, Hartford, Connecticut

POINTS

COMBINED POINTS

A DESIGNING MAN

In addition to being our third president, Thomas Jefferson was also an architect. Which of these buildings was *not* designed by him?

A. Monticello, Charlottesville, Virginia
B. James Barbour estate, Barboursville, Virginia
C. Carlyle House, Alexandria, Virginia
D. The Rotunda, University of Virginia, Charlottesville, Virginia
E. Virginia State Capitol, Richmond, Virginia

ANSWER: C

POINTS

A LONG WAY FROM HOME

Born in Maine, John Ford (1895–1973) won four Academy Awards. Which of the following movies was *not* directed by Ford?

A. *The Informer* (1935)
B. *Stagecoach* (1939)
C. *The Grapes of Wrath* (1940)
D. *How Green Was My Valley* (1941)
E. *The Third Man* (1949)
F. *The Quiet Man* (1952)

ANSWER: E

POINTS

WHEN IN ROME

How many of these facts about Roman antiquities did you know?

* The Romans copied from conquered territories
* Greek styles influenced their architecture
* Homes and public buildings have mosaic floors, sculpture, and colorful murals
* Roman craftsmen strove to create naturalistic paintings and portraits
* Roman painters developed the landscape genre and promoted *trompe l'oeil* as a style

POINTS

THE RENAISSANCE MAN

How many of these Renaissance buildings have you seen?

* Villa Capra, Vincenza, Italy
* Palais de Fontainebleau, Fontainebleau, France
* San Lorenzo de El Escorial, Madrid
* Jones's Banqueting House, London
* Saint Paul's Cathedral, London

POINTS

COMBINED POINTS

CHRISTIANITY REVS UP ITS INFLUENCE

Did you know these facts about early Christian iconography?

* The use of icons is characteristic of Byzantine (306 to 1453) art
* Icons were small images of Christ, the Virgin and Child, or a saint
* Because they were small, icons were often richly symbolic and detailed
* The Iconoclastic Controversy raged for several centuries in the Byzantine Empire as iconoclasts ("icon-smashers") objected to the depiction of religious images

POINTS

QUARTER CENTURY CLUB

The American Institute of Architects grants a Twenty-five Year Award for "an architectural design that has stood the test of time for 25 years." Can you pick out the winners from this list?

A. John Hancock Tower, Boston
B. Faneuil Hall Marketplace, Boston
C. Empire State Building, New York City
D. Vietnam Veterans Memorial, Washington, D.C.
E. Inland Steel Building, Chicago
F. East Building, National Gallery of Art, Washington, D.C.

ANSWER: A, B, D, F

POINTS

TAKE A KNEE

Can you name the location of each of these architecturally important church buildings?

1. Notre Dame
2. La Sagrada Familia
3. Church of Hallgrímur
4. St. Basil's Cathedral
5. Thorncrown Chapel
6. Ely Cathedral

ANSWER:

1. Paris
2. Barcelona
3. Reykjavik, Iceland
4. Moscow
5. Eureka Springs, Arkansas
6. Ely, England

POINTS

COMBINED POINTS

LOOKING BACKWARD

Which of the following postmodern buildings have you seen?

* AT&T Long Distance Building, New York City, with its "Chippendale" pediment
* Swan and Dolphin Hotel, Walt Disney World, Florida, designed by Michael Graves
* Engineering Research Center, University of Cincinnati, with sculptural smokestacks
* Vanna Venturi House, Philadelphia, by Robert Venturi
* Walt Disney Concert Hall, Los Angeles

POINTS

LET IT GROW

Organic architecture, a term coined by Frank Lloyd Wright, is exemplified in the following buildings. How many have you seen?

* The "Onion House" in Kona, Hawaii, designed by Kendrick Bangs Kellogg
* The National Farmers' Bank, Owatonna, Minnesota, designed by Louis Sullivan
* First and Second Goetheanums, Dornach, Switzerland, designed by Rudolf Steiner
* Sydney Opera House, Sydney, Australia, designed by Jorn Utzon
* The First Universalist Church in Rochester, New York, designed by Claude Fayette Bragdon

POINTS

COMBINED POINTS

IT'S ABOUT TIME

Which of the following did not occur or did *not* influence Renaissance thought and art?

1. The rediscovery of classical texts, which had been lost to the West for centuries
2. New access to mathematics and scientific advances from the Islamic world
3. Rise of the wealthy Medici family in Florence and their patronage of the arts
4. Increased influence of the Catholic church in the lives of individuals
5. Development of movable type in printing and the spread of printed works

ANSWER: 4. Increased influence of the Catholic church

POINTS

TO YOUR POST

Postmodern architecture seeks to break with modernist conventions. Did you know that:

* Postmodernism returns ornamentation to a building's façade
* Modernists criticize postmodern buildings as vulgar and cluttered with trinkets
* Modernists emphasize minimal use of materials and an absence of ornamentation
* Postmodern buildings often use a gable roof rather than the flat roof associated with modernism
* Postmodernists viewed the functionalism of modernists as boring and unwelcoming

POINTS

COMBINED POINTS

MICHELANGELO

How many of these facts about Michelangelo did you know?

* He gained knowledge of anatomy from studying corpses at a Florence church hospital
* Michelangelo tried to pass off a sculpture as ancient and the fraud was discovered
* Michelangelo's birth name was Michelangelo di Lodovico Buonarroti Simoni
* The *Pietà* was commissioned by a French cardinal as his funeral monument

POINTS

DONATELLO

Did you know these reasons the sculptor Donatello had such an influence on art?

* Donatello conducted the first archaeological study of Roman ruins in 1404
* Donatello's work moves away from the earlier period with attitudes of natural poise
* Donatello created three-dimensional depth on a two-dimensional surface
* He used scientific linear perspective developed by architect Brunelleschi

POINTS

A REAL RENAISSANCE MAN

How many of these facts about Leonardo da Vinci did you know?

* His expertise included painting, sculpture, architecture, music, science, mathematics, engineering, inventing, anatomy, geology, cartography, and botany.
* The *Mona Lisa* is in the Louvre because King Francis I invited da Vinci to live in France
* The *Mona Lisa* exemplifies his mastery of the *sfumato* technique of subtle contrasts
* A knowledge of mathematics helped the dramatic perspective of *The Last Supper*

POINTS

COMBINED POINTS

RAPHAEL

Which of the following items are true about Raphael, the third member of the High Renaissance trinity?

A. Raphael's paintings are considered the most serene and graceful of all three masters
B. He died in 1520 at age thirty-seven
C. He left very few completed works
D. He was commissioned by Pope Julius II to paint frescoes in the Vatican Palace
E. His masterpiece is *Stanza della Segnatura*

ANSWER: A, B, D, and E

POINTS

SUCCESS

Which of the following characteristics made the 1903 film *The Great Train Robbery* notable?

A. The film was the industry's first great box-office success
B. It established a star that the filmgoing public wanted to see in other movies
C. It is credited as having established the realistic narrative as a dominant form
D. Its popularity encouraged industry investment and permanent theaters countrywide
E. It also helped establish the average length of a film at twelve minutes

ANSWER: A, C, D, and E

POINTS

COMBINED POINTS

THE BIG EASY

How many of these historic New Orleans sites have you visited?

* Longue Vue House and Gardens
* Pitot House in Bayou St. John
* U.S. Custom House
* Doullet Houses in Holy Cross
* Shotgun houses throughout the city

POINTS

THE BIG APPLE

How many of these architecturally impressive buildings in New York City have you seen?

* IAC Headquarters
* 120 Wall Street
* Empire State Building
* Flatiron Building
* New Museum of Contemporary Art
* Woolworth Building
* St. Paul's Chapel

POINTS

BEANTOWN

Have you seen some of the most impressive architecture Boston has to offer?

* Boston Public Library
* Shad Hall, Harvard Business School
* Class of 1959 Chapel, Harvard Business School
* Federal Reserve Building
* Carpenter Center (Cambridge)—Le Corbusier's only North American building
* Kresge Chapel at MIT (Cambridge)

POINTS [   ]

COMBINED POINTS [   ]

THEY DON'T MAKE THEM ANYMORE

Frank Capra (1897–1991) is most famous for his films from the 1930s and 1940s. Have you seen the following?

* *It Happened One Night* (1934)
* *Mr. Deeds Goes to Town* (1936)
* *Lost Horizon* (1937)
* *You Can't Take It with You* (1938)
* *It's a Wonderful Life* (1946)

POINTS

WHAT MANNERS

The period of Mannerism emerged at the end of the High Renaissance (about 1520) in Rome and Florence. Did you know these facts?

* "Mannerism" derives from the Italian word *maniera* or "style"
* Mannerism emphasized sophistication and artificial qualities in reaction to naturalism
* Parmigianino epitomized Mannerism in *Madonna with the Long Neck*
* Tintoretto's *Last Supper* employs a carefully devised setting and dramatic light

POINTS

ON THE BANKS OF THE MOSKVA

Have you heard of these new architecturally interesting buildings in Moscow?

* Hermitage Plaza office complex
* The Red Guest Houses
* Molochnyi Dom apartment building
* Mercury Theatre
* Peter Fomenko's Workshop performing arts center
* Copper House residential and office complex

POINTS

COMBINED POINTS

NOT JUST PRETTY PICTURES

Early America was home to multi-talented artists who combined art with wider interests. Can you name what these artists are known for?

1. Charles Willson Peale (1741–1827)
2. John James Audubon (1785–1851)
3. George Catlin (1796–1872)

ANSWER:

1. Peale was a naturalist.
2. Audubon combined his knowledge of biology and botany with skill in drawing to encourage preservationism.
3. Catlin specialized in portraits of Native Americans.

POINTS

CAN YOU SEE ME NOW

Which four of the five structures on the list below are the tallest buildings in the world?

A. Burj Dubai, Dubai, United Arab Emirates
B. Taipei 101, Taipei, Taiwan
C. Shanghai World Financial Center, Shanghai, China
D. Willis Tower, Chicago
E. Petronas Towers, Kuala Lumpur, Malaysia

ANSWER: A, B, C, and E

POINTS

MORE EXPERIMENTING

Edwin S. Porter was perhaps the first important American film director. Did you know these facts about him?

* While Méliès never moved his camera, Porter was more innovative
* He made multi-scene narratives based on contemporary events
* His *Pan-American Exposition by Night* (1901) used time-lapse photography
* Porter's *Life of an American Fireman* (1903) used parallel editing
* His film *The Great Train Robbery* (1903) used other new techniques and continuity of action

POINTS

COMBINED POINTS

A BURGEONING INDUSTRY

For working- and middle-class audiences, motion pictures became extremely popular in the early twentieth century. Did you know the following?

* By 1910, more than 26 million people flocked to the movies each week in the United States
* Huge theaters were built, such as the 3,300-seat Strand Theatre on Broadway in New York City, which opened in 1914
* There were 21,000 movie theaters in the United States by 1916
* People began paying premium prices for longer, multiple-reel, feature films
* The studio system was born

POINTS

NEW ART FOR A NEW AMERICA

As our new nation developed, so did its artistic traditions. Can you match these early American works with the artist?

A. Benjamin West
B. John Singleton Copley
C. Gilbert Stuart
D. John Trumbull

1. *The Athenaeum* (1796)
2. *The Battle of Bunker Hill* (1786)
3. *Watson and the Shark* (1778)
4. *The Death of General Wolfe* (1770)

ANSWER: A, 4; B, 3; C, 1; D, 2

POINTS

CALIFORNIA CALLS

The popularity of movies in America brought with it changes to the industry. Were you aware of these facts?

* The demand for films meant that studios had to produce year-round
* In the early twentieth century, most movies were still shot outdoors using available light
* This made New York and Chicago, the original shooting locations, unsuitable
* In Hollywood, production companies found the climate and labor supply they needed

POINTS

COMBINED POINTS

COMMITTEES AT WORK

There are many beautiful and dramatic civic buildings that have been newly constructed in the United States. Have you seen these?

* U.S. Courthouse, Alpine, Texas
* Mattapan Branch, Boston Public Library, Boston
* Baldwin Hills Scenic Overlook, Culver City, California
* Charles Benenson Visitor Center and Gallery, Ghent, New York
* James Clarkson Environmental Discovery Center, White Lake, Michigan
* Neighborhood Resource Center, Phoenix

POINTS

ART RAISED IN AMERICA

How many of these works from the mid-nineteenth century Hudson River School have you seen?

* Thomas Cole's *The Garden of Eden* (1828)
* Asher Durand's *Kindred Spirits* (1849)
* Frederic Edwin Church's *The Heart of the Andes* (1859)
* Church's *Morning in the Tropics* (1877)

POINTS

STARRING THE FAMILY

Francis Ford Coppola (b. 1939) started as a screenwriter and co-wrote *Patton* (1970). Have you seen these Coppola films?

* *The Godfather* (1972)
* *The Conversation* (1974)
* *The Godfather Part II* (1974)
* *Apocalypse Now* (1979)

POINTS

COMBINED POINTS

A BIG COUNTRY

The American landscape inspired many landscape painters who ventured West. Are you familiar with the following?

* German-born Albert Bierstadt brought qualities of luminism into his grand creations
* Fitz Henry Lane's *Salem Harbor* (1853)
* Hudson River painters were some of the first professional artists trained in America
* Thomas Moran's paintings inspired the creation of the National Park Service

POINTS

AMERICA SOBERS UP

Did you know these facts about post–Civil War American artist Winslow Homer?

* Winslow Homer was unsentimental in such works as *Camp Fire* (1878)
* Homer is best known for his seascapes like *Breezing Up* (1876)
* Homer also popularized watercolor with such works as *Rowing Home* (1890)

POINTS

BETTER TO BE SEEN

Philip Johnson built his Glass House, a National Trust Historic Site, in New Canaan, Connecticut. Are you aware of these features of the site and know when it was built?

* The Brick House, almost completely enclosed by brick, contains living areas
* Johnson designed the Sculpture Gallery with a glass ceiling and five levels
* An underground Painting Gallery includes works by Stella, Warhol, and Rauschenberg
* The Library/Study is a freestanding building of less than 400 square feet
* The house was originally built in _____

ANSWER: 1949

POINTS

COMBINED POINTS

REALISM, REDUX

Can you name when American realist Thomas Eakins painted these important works?

1. *Max Schmitt in a Single Scull*
2. *The Gross Clinic*
3. *The Chess Players*
4. *The Swimming Hole*
5. *Portrait of Maud Cook*

ANSWER:

1. 1871
2. 1875
3. 1876
4. 1884–1885
5. 1895

POINTS

CITY OF ANGELS

Have you seen these examples of stunning architecture, old and new, in Los Angeles?

* Bradbury Building (1893)
* Caltrans District 7 headquarters (2004)
* Cathedral of Our Lady of the Angels (2002)
* The Getty Center (2006)
* Broad Contemporary Art Museum (2008)
* Los Angeles Design Center (2003)

POINTS

CITY BY THE BAY

How many of these exceptional San Francisco buildings have you seen?

* Cathedral of Christ the Light
* Contemporary Jewish Museum
* California Academy of Sciences
* U.S. Federal Building
* De Young Museum
* Port of San Francisco Ferry Building

POINTS

COMBINED POINTS

PICTURE THIS

American Alfred Stieglitz (1864–1946) helped photography become accepted as an art form. Have you seen these works and can you name another artist he helped popularize?

* *The Terminal* and *Winter – Fifth Avenue* were early works that earned him acclaim
* He produced *A Venetian Canal* and *A Wet Day on the Boulevard, Paris* while on his honeymoon
* *The Steerage* (1907) is considered his signature image
* In 1916, he met and started a long relationship with _____

ANSWER: Georgia O'Keeffe

POINTS

RISING AGAIN

As a dynamic city, Atlanta has many architectural gems. Have you seen the following?

* High Museum
* Fox Theatre
* Ivy Hall
* 1180 Peachtree
* Chandler Building
* Bank of America Plaza
* Margaret Mitchell House

POINTS

THE WINDY CITY

Which of the following is *not* one of the great buildings in Chicago?

A. The Modern Wing, Art Institute of Chicago
B. University of Chicago Booth School of Business
C. University of Chicago South Campus Chiller Plant
D. Chase Building
E. Chicago Public Library
F. Jay Pritzker Pavilion
G. Museum of Science and Industry
H. Merchandise Mart
I. Inland Steel Building

ANSWER: D

POINTS

COMBINED POINTS

AN ARTISTIC APPROACH

John Huston (1906–1987) studied as a painter and directed his films with an artistic vision. Have you seen these important Huston films?

* *The Maltese Falcon* (1941)
* *The Treasure of the Sierra Madre* (1948)
* *The Asphalt Jungle* (1950)
* *The African Queen* (1951)
* *The Misfits* (1961)

POINTS

TELLING THE TRUTH

The Ashcan School, an American realistic art movement, rose in the early twentieth century. How many Ashcan artists are you familiar with?

* Robert Henri sought journalistic art with his *Snow in New York* (1902)
* George Bellows painted the gritty boxing match *Dempsey and Firpo* (1924)
* John French Sloan created urban scenes such as *McSorley's Bar* (1912)
* Everett Shinn was another urban realist painter who painted *The Fight* (1899)

POINTS

BUCKEYES

The cities of Ohio boast examples of classic and contemporary architecture. Are you acquainted with the following?

* The Terminal Tower (Cleveland)
* BP Tower (Cleveland)
* Cincinnati Museum Center at Union Terminal (Cincinnati)
* Rosenthal Center for Contemporary Art (Cincinnati)
* Toledo Museum of Art (Toledo)
* Toledo Museum of Art Glass Pavilion (Toledo)

POINTS

COMBINED POINTS

AN ORIGINAL

Alfred Hitchcock (1899–1980) started directing films in Germany where he learned the techniques of Expressionism. Have you seen these films from the master of suspense?

* *Shadow of a Doubt* (1943)
* *Notorious* (1946)
* *Rear Window* (1954)
* *Vertigo* (1958)
* *North by Northwest* (1959)
* *Psycho* (1960)

POINTS

QUITE THE RESUME

Elia Kazan (1909–2003) directed on Broadway, produced, and wrote screenplays and novels. Are you familiar with these Kazan films?

* *Gentleman's Agreement* (1947)
* *A Streetcar Named Desire* (1951)
* *On the Waterfront* (1954)
* *East of Eden* (1955)
* *Splendor in the Grass* (1961)

POINTS

THE CITY OF FIRSTS

Baltimore has excellent examples of buildings representing a variety of architectural styles. Have you seen these?

* Baltimore Basilica
* Peale Museum
* Baltimore World Trade Center
* Brown Memorial Presbyterian Church
* Highfield House

POINTS

COMBINED POINTS

A DEPRESSING TIME

Walker Evans was an American photographer best known for documenting people and places during the Great Depression. Have you seen these important works?

* *View of Easton, Pennsylvania*
* *Street Scene, Morgan City, Louisiana*
* *Stable, Natchez, Mississippi*
* *View of Ossining, New York*
* *Alabama Tenant Farmer Wife*
* *Subway Passengers*

POINTS

GROUP F/64

How many of the photographs of Ansel Adams have you seen?

* *Glacier National Park*
* *Taos Pueblo*
* *Rose and Driftwood*
* *Clearing Winter Storm*
* *Moonrise, Hernandez, New Mexico*
* *Moon and Half Dome*

POINTS

ENVIRONMENTALLY SOUND

Can you name where these American Institute of Architects' Top Green projects are located?

1. First Unitarian Society Meeting House
2. Cherokee Studios housing project
3. Research Support Facility, Department of Energy National Renewable Energy Laboratory
4. LOTT Clean Water Alliance Regional Service Center

ANSWER:

1. Madison, Wisconsin
2. Los Angeles, California
3. Golden, Colorado
4. Olympia, Washington

POINTS

COMBINED POINTS

AMERICAN REALISM, REVISITED

Edward Hopper was a celebrated American realist who painted scenes of modern life. Are you familiar with these works?

* *Automat* (1927) is starkly and ambiguously moody
* *Chop Suey* (1929) depicts the play of light on two women in a restaurant
* *Gas* (1940) is another dramatic use of light, both natural and artificial
* His most famous work, showing careful control of shapes and lighting, is _____

ANSWER: *Nighthawks*

POINTS

A JOURNALISTIC APPROACH

David Lean (1908–1991) was born in England and worked as a film editor for newsreels. Have you seen these films directed by Lean?

* *Brief Encounter* (1945)
* *Great Expectations* (1946)
* *The Bridge on the River Kwai* (1957)
* *Lawrence of Arabia* (1962)
* *A Passage to India* (1984)

POINTS

AN EARLY START

George Stevens (1904–1975) started in the movie business as a cameraman when he was just seventeen years old. Do you know these Stevens films?

* *A Place in the Sun* (1951)
* *Shane* (1953)
* *Giant* (1956)
* *The Diary of Anne Frank* (1959)
* *The Greatest Story Ever Told* (1965)

POINTS

COMBINED POINTS

NOUVEAU ART

Have you seen these fine examples of Art Nouveau architecture?

* Historic Centre of Riga, Riga, Latvia
* Sagrada Familia Cathedral, Barcelona, Spain
* Eliseyev Emporium, St. Petersburg, Russia
* Grand Palais, Paris

POINTS

SCENE IN BOSTON

How many of these Boston-area art museums have you visited?

* Museum of Fine Arts
* Institute of Contemporary Art
* Isabella Stewart Gardner Museum
* Harvard Art Museums (Fogg, Busch-Reisinger, Sackler; all in Cambridge)
* MIT List Visual Arts Center (Cambridge)
* Peabody Essex Museum (Salem)
* deCordova Sculpture Park and Museum (Lincoln)

POINTS

GOOD IMPRESSIONS

How many of these post-impressionist artists' works are you familiar with?

* Vincent van Gogh's *Starry Night*
* Paul Gauguin's *Tahitian Women on the Beach*
* Georges Seurat's *A Sunday Afternoon on the Island of La Grande Jatte*
* Henri de Toulouse-Lautrec's *At the Moulin Rouge*
* Paul Cezanne's *The Bathers*

POINTS

COMBINED POINTS

SOME LIKE IT WILDER

Billy Wilder (1906–2002) enjoyed success as a screenwriter and producer in addition to director. Have you seen these acclaimed Wilder films?

- *Double Indemnity* (1944)
- *The Lost Weekend* (1945)
- *Sunset Boulevard* (1950)
- *Some Like It Hot* (1959)
- *Irma La Douce* (1963)

POINTS [　　　]

GONE BUT NOT FORGOTTEN

William Wyler (1902–1981) was an Academy Award–winning director. Have you seen these Wyler movies?

- *Wuthering Heights* (1939)
- *Mrs. Miniver* (1942)
- *The Best Years of Our Lives* (1946)
- *The Heiress* (1949)
- *Ben-Hur* (1959)

POINTS [　　　]

TOP TEN MOST INFLUENTIAL BUILDINGS OF THE TWENTIETH CENTURY

Can you name the architect of each of these famous twentieth-century buildings?

1. Villa Savoye
2. Barcelona Pavilion
3. Bauhaus School
4. Fallingwater
5. Parc de la Villette
6. Greater Columbus Convention Center
7. Seattle Public Library

ANSWER:

1. Le Corbusier
2. Ludwig Mies van der Rohe
3. Walter Gropius
4. Frank Lloyd Wright
5. Bernard Tschumi
6. Peter Eisenman
7. Rem Koolhaas

POINTS

COMBINED POINTS

STUDYING ABROAD

The 1800s brought more affordable travel and Americans studied art abroad. Which of the following nineteenth century American paintings have you seen?

* James McNeill Whistler produced *Symphony in White, No. 1: The White Girl* (1862)
* Whistler's *Nocturne in Black and Gold: The Falling Rocket* (1875)
* Mary Cassatt created the impressionistic *Summertime* (1894)
* John Singer Sargent created the bold *Portrait of Madame X* (1884)

POINTS

A NEW LINE OF WORK

Fred Zinnemann (1907–1997) was born in Vienna, studied law, and came to America to study film. Are you familiar with these Zinnemann films?

* *The Search* (1948)
* *High Noon* (1952)
* *From Here to Eternity* (1953)
* *A Man for All Seasons* (1966)
* *The Day of the Jackal* (1973)

POINTS

CINEMA FRANÇAIS

François Truffaut was one of the founders of French New Wave cinema.
How many of these Truffaut movies have you seen?

* *The 400 Blows* (1959)
* *Shoot the Piano Player* (1960)
* *Jules and Jim* (1962)
* *Fahrenheit 451* (1966)

POINTS

COMBINED POINTS

PRESERVATION HALLS

How many of these examples of architectural preservation and reuse have you seen?

* Ames Boston Hotel, Boston, Massachusetts
* Bryant Arts Center, Granville, Ohio
* Armstrong Oil and Gas headquarters, Denver, Colorado
* PNC Bank, Harbor East Branch, Baltimore, Maryland
* The Ford Assembly Building, Richmond, California
* Alameda Theatre, Alameda, California
* The Brant Foundation Art Study Center, Greenwich, Connecticut

POINTS

A NOUVEAU CENTURY

Art Nouveau was marked by stylish eroticism. Can you match the artist and the work?

A. Gustav Klimt
B. Alphonse Mucha
C. René Lalique
D. Tiffany
E. Aubrey Beardsley

1. Glasswork
2. *Judith and the Head of Holofernes*
3. Poster of Maude Adams as Joan of Arc
4. *The Peacock Skirt*
5. Windows, Brown Memorial Presbyterian Church, Baltimore

ANSWER: A, 2; B, 3; C, 1; D, 5; E, 4

POINTS

AMERICAN STYLE

Which of these post–World War II painters are you familiar with?

* Grant Wood's *American Gothic* (1930) has become an iconic twentieth-century image
* Thomas Hart Benton created *America Today* murals (1930–1931) and also created folksy murals for the Missouri State Capitol
* John Steuart Curry painted scenes from Kansas such as *Baptism in Kansas* (1928)

POINTS

THROUGH THE GLASS CEILING

Georgia O'Keeffe was the first woman artist to have a retrospective exhibit at MOMA; are you acquainted with her following works?

* *Blue and Green Music* (1921) is one of her innovative abstract images
* *Petunia No. 2* (1924) was her first large-scale flower painting
* *The Lawrence Tree* (1929) was completed after O'Keeffe moved to New Mexico
* *Summer Days* (1936) is a New Mexico landscape with a cow's skull and flowers

POINTS

COMBINED POINTS

READ ALL ABOUT IT

Which of the following art-oriented magazines do you read regularly?

* *The Believer*
* *Creative Review*
* *Esopus*
* *Film Comment*
* *American Craft*
* *Bidoun*

POINTS

SPACE PROGRAMS

Have you visited these recently completed American art museum additions?

* Bloch Building, Nelson-Atkins Museum of Art, Kansas City, Missouri
* Quadracci Pavilion, Milwaukee Art Museum, Milwaukee, Wisconsin
* The Walters Art Museum Renovation and Addition, Baltimore, Maryland
* Frederic C. Hamilton Building, Denver Art Museum, Denver, Colorado
* Teel Family Pavilion, Crocker Art Museum, Sacramento, California

POINTS

NEW WAVER

Jean-Luc Godard was another director of the New Wave school. Have you seen these Godard films?

* *Breathless* (1960)
* *Contempt* (1963)
* *La Chinoise* (1967)
* *Week End* (1967)

POINTS

KUROSAWA, FRAMED

Famed Japanese film director Akira Kurosawa based several of his movies on classic Western works. Pair up the works to the films.

A. *Ran*
B. *Hakuchi*
C. *Throne of Blood*
D. *Donzoko*

1. *The Lower Depths* by Gorky
2. *The Idiot* by Dostoevsky
3. *Macbeth* by Shakespeare
4. *King Lear* by Shakespeare

ANSWER: A, 2; B, 4; C, 1; D, 3

POINTS

COMBINED POINTS

SCORING YOURSELF:
ART AND ARCHITECTURE

Based on your responses to the checklists in the preceding section, use the rating system below to determine how you stand as an artistic intellectual.

0–21: You need to open your eyes to the world around you.

22–43: Your knowledge of art and architecture might impress the unlearned.

44–65: You have acquired an impressive artistic sensibility.

66–86: You must be an artistic genius.

Chapter 2

Literature

The Literature checklists following touch on a tiny but eclectic selection of literary works, people, and events. You'll be asked about authors from Homer to Faulkner and works from the *Iliad* to *Moonwalking with Einstein*.

As you read through these checklists, award yourself one point for correctly identifying all the elements in a checklist or for correctly answering the question posed. At the end of the section you'll have the opportunity to rate how intellectual you are on this subject.

A HOMER FOR THE GREEK TEAM

The Bible and Homer are the two primary sources of the tradition of Western literature. Did you know the following?

* Two epic poems are attributed to Homer: the *Iliad* and the *Odyssey*
* Both poems concern the Trojan War, an important focus of Greek history
* They introduce memorable human characters as well as Greek gods
* Homer's themes of peace and immortal glory have become a tradition in Western literature

POINTS

NO ID

Homer's life is largely a mystery although his contributions to literature are real. Did you know these facts about Homer?

* Nothing is known of Homer or his life
* He is believed to have flourished in the ninth or eighth century B.C.
* He may have come from Ionia (in modern Turkey) due to the Ionic dialect of the poems

POINTS

WORKS OF GREAT SIGNIFICANCE

The *Iliad* and the *Odyssey* are considered the most significant poems of the European tradition. Which of the following does *not* apply to the poems?

A. Modern scholars are skeptical that Homer was the author of the two poems
B. The epics were meant to be sung
C. Homer may have been responsible for first writing down a traditional oral narrative
D. There is evidence that the poems were the basis for stage performances
E. These two epics are the basis of Greek education throughout the Classical age

ANSWER: D

POINTS

COMBINED POINTS

TRAVELING MAN

The *Odyssey* concerns the period following the Trojan War. Do you know the following about this epic poem?

* Without the battle scenes of the *Iliad*, the *Odyssey* is less expressive and dramatic
* The *Odyssey* is more carefully crafted and harmoniously structured than the *Iliad*
* The story of the *Odyssey* is one of triumph and frustration on a grand scale
* Unlike the impending doom at the end of the *Iliad*, the *Odyssey* ends with reconciliation

POINTS

WHEN IN ROME

Much of Roman literature was largely derivative of Greek literature, but there were notable exceptions. Do you know the following about Virgil, considered the greatest of the Latin epic poets?

* Virgil is known for his long epic poems, the *Eclogues* and the *Georgics*
* His greatest work was the *Aeneid* (30 B.C.)
* Virgil worked on the *Aeneid* for the last ten years of his life
* By tradition, the work was commissioned by Augustus
* Both the *Odyssey* and *Iliad* are modeled in content and structure
* The poem is meant to glorify Rome and Augustus

POINTS

WAR STORY

Which of following statements about Homer's epic poem the *Iliad* are true?

1. The poem tells the story of the ten-year war between the Greeks and the people of Troy
2. The war dates from the ninth or tenth century B.C., but we know few details
3. In addition to telling the story of the lengthy war, the poem explores heroic ideals
4. The striving and frustrations of human characters are aided or blocked by intervention of the gods

ANSWER: Statements 1, 3, and 4 are true. Statement 2 is false; the war dates from the eleventh or twelfth century B.C.

POINTS

COMBINED POINTS

IT'S ALL GRECO-ROMAN TO ME

Match the name of the Greek god or goddess with the Roman equivalent.

A. Zeus	1. Ceres
B. Hera	2. Bacchus
C. Poseidon	3. Diana
D. Demeter	4. Venus
E. Athena	5. Neptune
F. Dionysus	6. Vulcan
G. Apollo	7. Minerva
H. Artemis	8. Mercury
I. Ares	9. Pluto
J. Aphrodite	10. Mars
K. Hephaestus	11. Jupiter
L. Hermes	12. Juno
M. Hades	13. Apollo

ANSWER: A, 11; B, 12; C, 5; D, 1; E, 7; F, 2; G, 13; H, 3; I, 10; J, 4; K, 6; L, 8; M, 9

POINTS

THE NINE CIRCLES OF HELL

Match the sin with the appropriate Circle of Hell from Dante's *Inferno*.

First Circle	Greed
Second Circle	Heresy
Third Circle	Lust
Fourth Circle	Treachery
Fifth Circle	Limbo
Sixth Circle	Anger
Seventh Circle	Violence
Eighth Circle	Gluttony
Ninth Circle	Fraud

ANSWER: First Circle, Limbo; Second Circle, Lust; Third Circle, Gluttony; Fourth Circle, Greed; Fifth Circle, Anger; Sixth Circle, Heresy; Seventh Circle, Violence; Eighth Circle, Fraud; Ninth Circle, Treachery

POINTS

COMBINED POINTS

THE BARD

Although Shakespeare, perhaps the greatest author in the English language, may be fading into the historical distance, he continues to throw his significant weight in literary circles. Are you familiar with the following?

* Born in 1564, William Shakespeare married twenty-six-year-old Anne Hathaway when he was eighteen
* In London, Shakespeare was competing with a new breed of playwright
* These "University Wits" created works with historical characters in a poetic style
* Christopher Marlowe was one of the Wits
* Shakespeare joined an acting company and wrote his first plays in about 1590

POINTS

SUCCESS

Whether it was Shakespeare's plays or some other cause, Lord Chamberlain's Men were successful. Did you know the following?

* The company built its own theater, the Globe, in 1599
* Queen Elizabeth died in 1603 and was succeeded by James I
* James ordered Shakespeare's company to change its name to the King's Men
* Shakespeare was able to buy a large house in Stratford

POINTS

FATE TAKES A HAND

Did you know the following about the last decade of the sixteenth century?

* In 1592, an outbreak of a disease forced all theaters in London to close. What was the disease? _____
* Shakespeare wrote *Richard III* and *The Taming of the Shrew* at this time
* He also started writing poetry
* Theaters reopened in 1594 and Shakespeare joined the Lord Chamberlain's Men company
* Only this company performed Shakespeare's plays

ANSWER: The plague

POINTS

COMBINED POINTS

ALL HIS WORLD WAS A STAGE

Part of Shakespeare's reputation rests on his prodigious output. Were you aware of these facts?

- Shakespeare produced thirty-eight plays in twenty-four years
- Despite his popularity, he was unheralded at the time of his death in 1616
- Shakespearean plays are particularly rich with imagery and complex themes
- He employed prologues and epilogues delivered directly to the audience
- Double entendres, comic events, and instances of mistaken identity relieve tension

POINTS

ENDURANCE

Shakespeare is still popular with audiences and his work provides a rite of passage for serious actors and actresses. His continued appeal can be traced to the following:

- The poetic beauty of his imagery and language
- The narrative drive of his plays
- His psychologically rich, memorable characters
- His contextual sensitivity to the nuances of life

POINTS

VERSIFICATION

Shakespeare was responsible for some of the most beautiful poetry in the English language. Did you know the following about his verse?

* Sonnets are fourteen-line poems that originated in Renaissance Italy
* Shakespeare wrote about (A) 50, (B) 100, (C) 150, or (D) 250 sonnets?
* Many of his sonnets are addressed to or are about a young man
* Twenty-five of the sonnets are addressed to or are about a "dark lady"
* Critics now consider his sonnets "verbal contraptions" concerned with moral issues

ANSWER: C

POINTS

COMBINED POINTS

ALL THE BETTER TO UNDERSTAND YOU WITH

How many of the following facts about our language do you know?

* What's considered modern English dates from the fifteenth century
* The changes from Middle English are known as the "Great Vowel Shift"
* The reasons for this change remain a mystery
* Some scholars believe that plagues caused population and language shifts

POINTS

A SOUND IDEA

Throughout history, various learned people have attempted to purify language. Are you aware of the following events that attempted to standardize the English language?

* London's Royal Society formed a group in 1622 "to improve the English tongue"
* The group hoped to establish a body along the lines of the Académie française
* That committee produced nothing and another attempt was made in 1712
* Politics foiled the second effort and the plan was abandoned

POINTS

A DREAM REALIZED

The English critic and essayist Samuel Johnson was able to accomplish, almost single-handedly, what the Royal Society did not. Did you know the following?

* His *A Dictionary of the English Language* was published in 1755
* It included 40,000 words and 114,000 illustrative quotations
* It took Johnson eight years—along with six assistants—to complete the work
* The Académie française took _____ years and forty people to publish its dictionary

ANSWER: forty

POINTS

COMBINED POINTS

ONCE MORE WITH FEELING

By 1857, the Philological Society of London concluded that a new dictionary was needed. Are you aware of the following events?

* In 1879, an agreement was reached with James Murray to create a new dictionary
* Plans called for a four-volume work to be completed in ten years
* Work on the reference actually took forty-nine years
* Murray's *A New English Dictionary on Historical Principles* encompassed ten volumes

POINTS

DEFINITIVE, OR NOT

Work began on updating Murray's definitive dictionary almost immediately. Did you know:

* In 1993, the dictionary expanded to twelve volumes and one supplement
* It was renamed the *Oxford English Dictionary* and filled 15,000 pages
* A new edition, made up of twenty volumes, was published in 1989
* The online version of the *OED* adds words on a regular basis

POINTS

ACROSS THE POND

The English language was getting a workout in America as well, responding to unique conditions and requirements. Did you know the following?

* Early English settlers' speech was augmented by Indian terms for new plants and animals
* Expansion and the influx of cultures brought loanwords from many languages
* In 1806, Noah Webster published his first dictionary of American English
* His two-volume dictionary in 1828 fixed spellings and established grammar rules
* His work, while not a commercial success, was highly influential on the language

POINTS

COMBINED POINTS

KEEPING UP

There is no official mechanism for adding words to the English language. Were you aware of the ways our language changes?

* Dictionary publishers review the thousands of newly coined words every year
* New words come most frequently from the areas of science, business, and popular culture
* The American Dialect Society has designated a word of the year since 1991
* Some linguists believe that it requires two generations for a word to prove its durability

POINTS

BOOK 'EM

Which of these are included in your personal library?

* A first edition
* A book of poetry by a single author
* An autographed book
* A leather-bound edition

POINTS

GETTING STARTED

William Cullen Bryant (1794–1878) was one of the first American romantic poets. Did you know these facts about him?

* He wrote "Thanatopsis" in 1811 when he was seventeen years old
* This romantic poem inspired Ralph Waldo Emerson and Henry David Thoreau
* He practiced law and was editor of the *New York Evening Post* for fifty years
* He was inspired to write "To a Waterfowl" while walking to his law practice

POINTS

COMBINED POINTS

A POET FOR HIS TIME

Henry Wadsworth Longfellow (1807–1882) also was an American romantic poet as well as an educator. Which of the following is *not* true about his life and work?

A. He was a professor at Bowdoin College and Harvard College
B. He wrote mostly lyric poetry, known for its musicality
C. Longfellow's poetry was immensely popular during his lifetime
D. His works include "Evangeline," "The Song of Hiawatha," and "Paul Revere's Ride"
E. Today his work is considered some of the most original verse written to date

ANSWER: E

POINTS

A NATURAL

Walt Whitman (1819–1892) was an influential and controversial American poet and essayist. Did you know these facts about him?

* Whitman finished his formal education at age eleven
* He was influenced by the Transcendentalists, but also incorporated realism in his work
* He served as a nurse in Army hospitals during the Civil War
* Whitman is known as America's first "poet of democracy" and the father of free verse

POINTS

LEAVES OF GRASS

Walt Whitman's best-known work is *Leaves of Grass*. Did you know these facts about the work?

* He wished to write an American epic and chose free verse and a Bible-based cadence
* He paid for the publication of the first edition of his collection of verse, *Leaves of Grass* (1855)
* Whitman continued to revise it through eight editions throughout his life
* Though the book was praised by Emerson, its overt sexuality was generally considered obscene
* Whitman denied being a homosexual, but today it is considered as part of his work

POINTS

COMBINED POINTS

A PRIVATE PERSON

Emily Dickinson was a nineteenth-century American poet who, after her education, remained a virtual recluse in her parents' home. Did you know the following?

* She admired the Transcendentalists and Romantic poets
* Her style was reminiscent of the English Metaphysical poets
* Her poetry used highly symbolic imagery, short lines, and unconventional punctuation
* Only ten of her nearly 1,800 poems were published during her lifetime
* Her family discovered forty hand-bound volumes of her poetry after her death

POINTS

AN ESTABLISHED VOICE

Did you know the following about American poet Robert Frost?

* Frost attended Dartmouth and Harvard, but never graduated
* An unsuccessful farmer, he turned to teaching at Amherst and Middlebury colleges
* Frost read his poetry at John F. Kennedy's inauguration in 1961
* Frost was known for his realistic rural scenes and colloquial speech
* Frost was awarded four Pulitzer prizes for poetry

POINTS

THE REALITY OF LIFE

The turn of the twentieth century, with its war, brought changes in the nation's mood. Were you aware of the effects on American poetry?

* The Modernist poets, or "lost generation," reflected the social disillusionment of the period
* Their verse used unusual imagery and unconventional poetic structure
* Ezra Pound developed Imagism, which favored clear images and precise language
* Pound's incomplete *The Cantos* covers many subjects in fifteen languages
* An important poem from this period is T. S. Eliot's *The Love Song of J. Alfred Prufrock*
* Eliot's *The Waste Land* is another stream-of-consciousness Modernist landmark

POINTS

COMBINED POINTS

FREE THINKING

William Carlos Williams was another American Modernist and Imagist poet. Did you know the following about Williams?

* Williams was a pediatrician who wrote poetry between appointments
* He met and was influenced by Ezra Pound and James Joyce on a trip to Europe in 1924
* In his work, Williams tried to portray everyday subjects with an experimental structure
* His "The Red Wheelbarrow" uses Imagist conventions to convey the objective representation of a wheelbarrow in sixteen words

POINTS

VERSE FOR TODAY

Modern poetry seems to be in search of an audience. Are you aware of the following?

* John Ashbery is an important voice of postmodern poetry
* His "Self-Portrait in a Convex Mirror" was published in 1975
* Other notable figures are Gwendolyn Brooks, Maya Angelou, Donald Hall, and Sylvia Plath
* Slam poetry events spotlight poetry's performance and vocal nature

POINTS

ALL OF ME

Which of the following prolific author's complete works have you read?

* William Faulkner
* Ernest Hemingway
* James Joyce
* William Shakespeare

POINTS

COMBINED POINTS

PRIZE NOVELS

How many of these *New York Times* best works of fiction of 2010 have you read?

* *Freedom* by Jonathan Franzen
* *The New Yorker Stories* by Ann Beattie
* *Room* by Emma Donoghue
* *Selected Stories* by William Trevor

POINTS

RECOMMENDED

How many of these *New York Times* best nonfiction books of 2010 have you read?

* *Cleopatra: A Life* by Stacy Schiff
* *The Emperor of All Maladies: A Biography of Cancer* by Siddhartha Mukherjee
* *Finish the Hat: Collected Lyrics* by Stephen Sondheim
* *The Warmth of Other Suns: The Epic Story of America's Great Migration* by Isabel Wilkerson

POINTS

NEW AND NOVEL

Have you read these Pulitzer Prize–winning novels?

* *A Visit from the Goon Squad* by Jennifer Egan
* *Tinkers* by Paul Harding
* *Olive Kitteridge* by Elizabeth Strout
* *The Brief Wondrous Life of Oscar Wao* by Junot Diaz
* *The Road* by Cormac McCarthy

POINTS

COMBINED POINTS

THE BEST OF HISTORY

How many of these Pulitzer Prize–winning history titles have you read?

* *The Fiery Trial: Abraham Lincoln and American Slavery* by Eric Foner
* *Lords of Finance: The Bankers Who Broke the World* by Liaquat Ahamed
* *The Hemingses of Monticello: An American Family* by Annette Gordon-Reed
* *What Hath God Wrought: The Transformation of America, 1815–1848* by Daniel Walker Howe
* *The Race Beat: The Press, the Civil Rights Struggle, and the Awakening of a Nation* by Gene Roberts and Hank Klibanoff

POINTS

THEY TAKE THE PRIZE

Have you read these Pulitzer Prize–winning general nonfiction books?

* *The Dead Hand: The Untold Story of the Cold War Arms Race and Its Dangerous Legacy* by David E. Hoffman
* *Slavery by Another Name: The Re-Enslavement of Black Americans from the Civil War to World War II* by Douglas A. Blackmon
* *The Years of Extermination: Nazi Germany and the Jews, 1939–1945* by Saul Friedländer
* *The Looming Tower: Al-Qaeda and the Road to 9/11* by Lawrence Wright

POINTS

LIVES IN INK

How many of these Pulitzer Prize–winning biographies or autobiographies have you read?

* *Washington: A Life* by Ron Chernow
* *The First Tycoon: The Epic Life of Cornelius Vanderbilt* by T. J. Stiles
* *American Lion: Andrew Jackson in the White House* by Jon Meacham
* *Eden's Outcasts: The Story of Louisa May Alcott and Her Father* by John Matteson
* *The Most Famous Man in America: The Biography of Henry Ward Beecher* by Debby Applegate

POINTS

COMBINED POINTS

POETIC LICENSE

Have you read this Pulitzer Prize–winning poetry?

* *The Best of It: New and Selected Poems* by Kay Ryan
* *Versed* by Rae Armantrout
* *The Shadow of Sirius* by W. S. Merwin
* *Time and Materials* by Robert Hass
* *Failure* by Philip Schultz

POINTS

GOOD HABITS

Do you . . .

* Subscribe to at least one daily newspaper?
* Visit the library at least twice per month?
* Support your local schools?

POINTS

BOOK LISTS

How many of these National Book Award winners for fiction have you read?

* *Lord of Misrule* by Jaimy Gordon
* *Let the Great World Spin* by Colum McCann
* *Shadow Country* by Peter Matthiessen
* *Tree of Smoke* by Denis Johnson
* *The Echo Maker* by Richard Powers

POINTS

COMBINED POINTS

READING WITH THE STARS

How many of these National Book Award nonfiction winners have you read?

* *Just Kids* by Patti Smith
* *Legacy of Ashes: The History of the CIA* by Tim Weiner
* *The Worst Hard Time: The Untold Story of Those Who Survived the Great American Dust Bowl* by Timothy Egan
* *The Year of Magical Thinking* by Joan Didion
* *Arc of Justice: A Saga of Race, Civil Rights, and Murder in the Jazz Age* by Kevin Boyle

POINTS

SUBSCRIBERS

How many of these literary magazines do you read regularly?

* *The Paris Review*
* *Tin House*
* *Ploughshares*
* *Southern Review*
* *New England Review*
* *The New Yorker*

POINTS

WHO WROTE THAT

Can you match these famous American authors with their work?

1. Henry David Thoreau
2. Louisa May Alcott
3. Upton Sinclair
4. Nathaniel Hawthorne
5. Henry James
6. Edith Wharton

A. *The Scarlet Letter*
B. *Walden*
C. *Ethan Frome*
D. *Little Women*
E. *The Jungle*
F. *The Portrait of a Lady*

ANSWER: 1, B; 2, D; 3, E; 4, A; 5, F; 6, C

POINTS

COMBINED POINTS

ABOUT PRESIDENTS

Which of these presidential biographies have you read?

* *Founding Father: Rediscovering George Washington* by Richard Brookhiser
* *John Adams* by David McCullough
* *Truman* by David McCullough
* *With Malice Toward None: A Life of Abraham Lincoln* by Stephen B. Oates
* *Coolidge: An American Enigma* by Robert Sobel
* *Camelot and the Cultural Revolution* by James Piereson
* *The Age of Reagan* by Steven Hayward
* *Alexander Hamilton* by Ron Chernow

POINTS

BY PRESIDENTS

Which of these presidential autobiographies have you read?

* *The Complete Personal Memoirs of Ulysses S. Grant* by Ulysses S. Grant
* *An American Life: The Autobiography* by Ronald Reagan
* *My Life* by Bill Clinton
* *Keeping Faith: Memoirs of a President* by Jimmy Carter
* *Theodore Roosevelt: An Autobiography* by Theodore Roosevelt
* *The Autobiography of Calvin Coolidge* by Calvin Coolidge

POINTS

WHAT DID HE SAY

Can you match these authors with their quotations about poetry?

1. Robert Louis Stevenson	A. Poetry comes nearer to vital truth than history
2. T. S. Eliot	B. Poetry expresses the universal, and history only the particular
3. John Donne	C. Genuine poetry can communicate before it is understood
4. Aristotle	D. Wine is bottled poetry
5. Plato	E. I am two fools, I know, for loving, and for saying so in whining poetry

ANSWER: 1, D; 2, C; 3, E; 4, B; 5, A

POINTS

COMBINED POINTS

THE BEST WORDS IN THE BEST ORDER

Can you define all of these poetic terms?

1. Assonance is _____
2. A caesura is _____
3. Consonance is _____
4. Enjambment is _____
5. An iamb is _____
6. A trochee is _____

ANSWER:

1. repetition of the same or similar vowel sounds
2. a pause in a line of poetry indicated naturally or by punctuation
3. repetition of the same or similar consonant sounds
4. the running on of a thought from one line to the next without a break
5. an unstressed syllable followed by a stressed syllable
6. a stressed syllable followed by an unstressed syllable

POINTS

AND THE ENVELOPE PLEASE

For which of these novels did William Faulkner receive the Pulitzer Prize?

* *The Sound and the Fury*
* *As I Lay Dying*
* *Light in August*
* *Absalom, Absalom!*
* *A Fable*
* *The Reivers*

ANSWER: *A Fable* and *The Reivers*

POINTS

PAGE-TURNERS

How many of these *New York Times* nonfiction bestselling books by intellectual authors have you read?

* *The Checklist Manifesto* by Atul Gawande
* *The Immortal Life of Henrietta Lacks* by Rebecca Skloot
* *Inside of a Dog* by Alexandra Horowitz
* *Moonwalking with Einstein* by Joshua Foer
* *Physics of the Future* by Michio Kaku
* *The Social Animal* by David Brooks
* *Unfamiliar Fishes* by Sarah Vowell

POINTS

COMBINED POINTS

SCORING YOURSELF: LITERATURE

Based on your responses to the checklists in the preceding section, use the rating system below to determine how you stand as a literary intellectual.

0–12: You need to get thee to a library and stay there for many a fortnight to make up for thy illiterate life.

13–25: You read enough to get by in college.

26–38: You have read enough books by intellectuals to be accepted in a book club run by Sarah Vowell.

39–50: You would be a worthy successor to the finest literary authors.

Chapter 3

Music

The Music checklists range from music theory to the latest developments in modern dance. Along the way you'll find checklists on the origins of opera, great orchestras, and Johnny B. Goode.

Give yourself one point if you correctly identify all the elements in a checklist or answer the question. At the end of the section you'll have the opportunity to rate how intellectual you are on this subject.

COMPOSITION IN BLACK AND WHITE

How many of these groups of instruments in a classical orchestra are you familiar with and how many examples do you know?

* Strings—violin, viola, cello, bass
* Woodwinds—clarinet, oboe, bassoon, flute
* Brass—trumpet, trombone, tuba
* Percussion—triangle, timpani

POINTS

LISTEN TO THIS

How many of these famous sonatas have you heard performed?

* *Devil's Trill Sonata* by Guiseppi Tartini
* *Piano Sonata No. 16 in C Major* by Wolfgang Amadeus Mozart
* *Piano Sonata No. 2 in B-flat Minor* by Frédéric Chopin

POINTS

THE CLASSICS

Can you define each of these classical music forms?

1. Chamber music
2. Concerto
3. Minuet
4. Sonata
5. Symphony

ANSWER:

1. *Chamber music* is meant to be played in a room by a small group of musicians
2. A *concerto* is a three-movement piece, written for an instrumental soloist and an accompanying orchestra
3. The *minuet* was originally used as a stately dance song, and then used as a third movement in a symphony
4. A *sonata* is a single (and usually the first) movement of a symphony; it has three parts
5. A *symphony* is a long piece that usually contains four movements

POINTS

COMBINED POINTS

STANDOUT CONCERTOS

Which of these concertos have you heard?

* *Piano Concerto in A Minor, Op.54* by Franz Schubert
* *Violin Concerto in D Major, Op. 61* by Ludwig van Beethoven
* *Piano Concerto No. 1 in E-flat Major, S.124* by Franz Liszt
* *Concerto for Piano and Wind Instruments* by Igor Stravinsky

POINTS

SCHOOL DAYS

Can you name the top ballet schools in New York, London, Milan, Moscow, and St. Petersburg?

ANSWER:

* School of American Ballet, New York
* Royal Ballet School, London
* La Scala Theatre Ballet School, Milan, Italy
* The Bolshoi Ballet Academy, Moscow
* Vaganova Academy of Russian Ballet, St. Petersburg, Russia

POINTS

EYEWITNESS

How many of the following great ballets have you seen?

* *La Bayadere*
* *Cinderella*
* *Le Corsaire*
* *Don Quixote*
* *Giselle*
* *The Nutcracker*
* *Romeo & Juliet*
* *The Sleeping Beauty*
* *Swan Lake*

POINTS

COMBINED POINTS

ON YOUR TOES

How many of these current ballet dancers have you seen perform?

* Carlos Acosta
* Alina Cojocaru
* Anthony Dowel
* Natalia Osipova
* Ivan Vasiliev

POINTS

STAGE STRUCK

At how many of these notable venues have you seen a ballet performed?

* American Ballet Theatre, New York
* The Bolshoi, Moscow
* New York City Ballet, New York
* Paris Opera Ballet, Paris
* The Royal Ballet, London
* La Scala, Milan, Italy

POINTS

THE BALLETOMANE'S VOCABULARY

Can you define each of the following ballet terms?

1. Ballon
2. Cabriole
3. Fondu
4. Glissade
5. Piqué
6. Relevé

ANSWER:

1. Bounce, the light, elastic quality in a dancer's jump
2. Caper, a step in which the legs are beaten in the air
3. Sinking down, lowering the body by bending the supporting knee
4. Glide, a traveling step
5. Pricked, stepping on the point of one foot with the other foot raised
6. Raised, raising the body on the points of both feet

POINTS

COMBINED POINTS

LESSON TIME

Which of the following celebrities do not have training in classical ballet?

* Naomi Campbell
* Anne Hathaway
* Elizabeth Moss
* Sarah Jessica Parker
* Jean-Claude Van Damme
* Michelle Yeoh

ANSWER: Anne Hathaway

POINTS

DID YOU KNOW

Do you know the following historical facts about ballet?

* Ballet started in fifteenth-century Italy as a dance interpretation of fencing
* The earliest modern ballet on record was performed in Milan in 1489
* Ballet was performed by French royalty during the seventeenth century
* Dancers' costumes were based on court dress; women wore tight corsets
* Male dancers' movements were less restricted

POINTS

EARLY DAYS

Early ballet followed the forms of other period arts. Did you know the following?

* Ballet technique favored symmetry and balance
* Dancers were encouraged to present painting-like tableaux
* Ballet d'action, emphasizing a dancer's movements, was introduced by Jean-Georges Noverre in 1760
* Noverre's *Les Horaces* was first presented in 1774 in Vienna

POINTS

COMBINED POINTS

HOW ROMANTIC

The rise of Romanticism in the early nineteenth century brought important changes to the ballet. Did you know the following facts about ballet of this period?

* The Paris staging of *Robert le Diable* (1831) featured a premier female dancer
* The performance of Marie Taglioni made her an international star
* Taglioni's grace replaced the former emphasis on male athleticism
* The *pointe* technique of toe dancing became established during this period

POINTS

THE SCENE SHIFTS

The late nineteenth century saw more changes in ballet. How many of the following events are you aware of?

* By the 1880s, ballet's inventiveness and popularity was in decline in Paris
* The czars of Russia became enthusiastic patrons of ballet at this time
* Two Russian choreographers, Marius Petipa and Lev Ivanov, came into prominence
* A trio of Tchaikovsky's ballets was staged between 1890 and 1895
* Russian dancers graduated from the classical Imperial Ballet School

POINTS

ANOTHER CENTURY

Russian influence on the ballet continued into the twentieth century. Did you know:

* Serge Diaghilev founded the influential Ballet Russes
* Ballet Russes's 1909 Paris performance astonished the Western ballet establishment
* Diaghilev hired the best choreographers, dancers, composers, and designers of the time
* Stravinsky was commissioned to write *The Firebird* and *The Rite of Spring*

POINTS

COMBINED POINTS

TRAIN SPOTTING

Which of the following is not a training method of ballet?

* Balanchine method (American)
* Cecchetti method (Italian)
* Stuttgart method (German)
* Royal Academy of Dance method (English)
* Vaganova method (Russian)

ANSWER: Stuttgart method

POINTS

SERGEIOUSLY

How many of the following ballets by Sergei Prokofiev have you seen?

* *Ala i Lolli*
* *Chout (The Tale of the Buffoon)*
* *Trapeze*
* *Le pas d'acier (The Steel Step)*
* *The Prodigal Son*
* *On the Dnieper*
* *Romeo and Juliet*
* *Cinderella*
* *The Tale of the Stone Flower*

POINTS

HARD CORE

How many of the following books on ballet do you own?

* *Apollo's Angels: A History of Ballet* by Jennifer Homans
* *The Cambridge Companion to Ballet,* edited by Marion Kant
* *Ballet in Western Culture* by Carol Lee
* *Ballet 101* by Robert Greskovic
* *101 Stories of the Great Ballets* by George Balanchine
* *The Ballet Companion* by Eliza Gaynor Minden

POINTS

COMBINED POINTS

ACCOMPANIED

Many ballet companies have long and storied histories, but some are new. Have you heard of these?

* The Australian Ballet gave its first performance in 1962
* The National Ballet of Canada was founded in 1951
* The Ballet Nacional de Cuba was founded in 1948

POINTS [   ]

DANCE TO THE MUSIC

Which pop music artist donated $250,000 to the American Ballet Theatre for its arts education program?

* Cher
* Prince
* Paul Simon
* Sting

ANSWER: Prince

POINTS [   ]

PIONEERING SPIRIT

How many of the following facts about Isadora Duncan did you know?

* Duncan is considered the most important pioneer in modern dance
* She believed that traditional ballet technique distorted the body's natural movement
* She called ballet dancers "articulated puppets"
* Duncan said that ballet separates body movements from the mind

POINTS

COMBINED POINTS

A NEW VISION

Isadora Duncan articulated her vision with new techniques. Did you know:

* Duncan was inspired by movements in nature, particularly the wind and waves
* Her dancing included upraised arm and head positions and flowing rhythmical movements
* She believed that dance should be the "divine expression" of the human spirit
* Her dance became more primitive and less fairy-tale like than ballet

POINTS

EXPRESSIVE MOVEMENTS

Do you know the following about these modern dance innovators?

* Martha Graham saw the back and pelvis as the center of movement
* Graham's characteristic movements included a spiral or arch of the back
* Doris Humphrey saw the importance of the transition between a fall and recovery
* Many of Mary Wigman's movements were completed near the floor

POINTS

VISIONING

Early modern dance portrayed expressive characteristics. Did you know:

* Early choreographers did not include the gravity-defying leaps of ballet
* Modern dance emphasized the strain of dancing rather than concealing it
* Martha Graham's work in particular showed the dancers' struggle and passion
* Movements were not decorative shapes but expressive gestures

POINTS

COMBINED POINTS

CHANGE AFOOT

Early twentieth-century modern dance was changing. Do you know the following?

* Merce Cunningham changed the face of dance in the 1940s
* He believed dance should be about itself—not narrative or emotional expression
* Cunningham's dance was independent of the music and design
* He believed any movement could be appropriate dance material
* He claimed that expression would rise out of the dance itself

POINTS

MORE CHANGES

In the 1960s and 1970s, new influences were felt in dance. Can you identify these changes?

* Postmodern choreographers wanted to take Cunningham's ideas further
* They felt that simpler structure would improve the clarity and enjoyment of dance
* Postmodernists used walking, skipping, and running movements
* Dancers wore street clothes, sets and lighting were minimal, and performances were not staged
* Postmodern dances did not portray narrative or expression

POINTS

GOTTA DANCE

How many of these dance companies have you seen in performance?

* Alvin Ailey American Dance Theater
* Mark Morris Dance Group
* Paul Taylor Dance Company
* Martha Graham Dance Company
* Twyla Tharp Dance

POINTS

COMBINED POINTS

THE BASIC REPERTOIRE

Did you know that these sounds were put on a gold record that was sent into space with the Voyager spacecraft in 1977?

* Baby sounds
* *Johnny B. Goode*
* Sounds of surf and wind
* J. S. Bach compositions

POINTS

MY STUDENT

Which of these composers did Haydn teach?

* Beethoven
* Brahms
* Mozart
* Schubert

ANSWER: Mozart

POINTS

AIRING IT OUT

Which of these famous opera arias have you heard performed?

* "E lucevan le stelle" from Puccini's *Tosca*
* "Che gelida manina" from Puccini's *La Boheme*
* "Nessun dorma" from Puccini's *Turandot*
* "Un bel di vedremo" from Puccini's *Madama Butterfly*
* "La donna e mobile" from Verdi's *Rigoletto*

POINTS

COMBINED POINTS

MUSICALLY INCLINED

Can you match the opera with the period in which it was composed?

A. Monteverdi's *Orpheus*

B. Mozart's *The Marriage of Figaro*

C. Verdi's *Rigoletto*

D. Britten's *Death in Venice*

1. Modern era

2. Baroque era

3. Romantic era

4. Classical era

ANSWER: A, 2; B, 4; C, 3; D, 1

POINTS

WORKS FOR ME

In which of these famous opera houses have you seen a performance?

* La Fenice, Venice, Italy
* Metropolitan Opera, New York City
* Paris Opéra *(Palais Garnier)*, Paris
* Royal Opera House, London
* La Scala (*Teatro alla Scala*), Milan, Italy
* Sydney Opera House, Sydney
* Vienna State Opera, Vienna

POINTS

TALK THE TALK

How many of these basic opera terms can you define?

1. Aria
2. Libretto
3. Opera
4. Recitative

ANSWER:

1. *Aria*, the second style of singing, is used to express emotions in an elaborate, structured melodic style
2. *Libretto* is the text of the opera, literally "little book"
3. *Opera* is the plural of Latin *opus*, or "work"
4. *Recitative* is one of two styles of singing in which the singer follows the rhythms of ordinary speech

POINTS

COMBINED POINTS

ANCIENT HISTORY

How many of the following facts about the history of opera do you know?

* Jacopo Peri's *Dafne,* performed in Florence in 1597, is considered to be the first opera
* Peri's *Euridice* (1600) is the earliest opera score to have survived
* The first opera still to be regularly performed is to Claudio Monteverdi's *L'Orfeo* (1607)
* The first public opera house opened in Venice in 1637

POINTS

EARLY TIMES

Most opera was presented to the court in the seventeenth and eighteenth centuries. Did you know the following?

* The staging of opera was critical; designers might receive greater acclaim than composers
* Darkening the theater was not a convention during this time
* The audience was part of the spectacle, with spectators following the action in a libretto
* Librettos were also part of the event and elaborately illustrated

POINTS

MOSTLY MOZART

Mozart composed all but which one of the following operas?

* *Die Zauberflöte (The Magic Flute)*
* *Die Entführung aus dem Serail (The Abduction from the Seraglio)*
* *Fidelio*
* *Così fan tutte*
* *Don Giovanni*

ANSWER: *Fidelio* was composed by Ludwig van Beethoven

POINTS

COMBINED POINTS

THAT'S NOT MINE

Richard Wagner was responsible for all but which of the following operas?

* *Der Fliegende Holländer (The Flying Dutchman)*
* *Tannhäuser*
* *Der Ring des Nibelungen (The Ring of the Nibelung)*
* *Der Rosenkavalier (The Knight of the Rose)*

ANSWER: *Der Rosenkavalier* was composed by Richard Strauss

POINTS

JOE GREEN

Giuseppe Verdi composed all but which of the following operas?

* *Rigoletto*
* *Il trovatore (The Troubadour)*
* *La traviata (The Fallen Woman)*
* *Otello*
* *Pagliacci (Clowns)*

ANSWER: *Pagliacci* was composed by Ruggero Leoncavallo

POINTS

MOTHER RUSSIA

Russian influence on the opera occurred largely in the nineteenth century. How many of these Russian operas have you seen?

* Modest Mussorgsky's *Boris Godunov*
* Pyotr Tchaikovsky's *Eugene Onegin*
* Sergei Prokofiev's *War and Peace*
* Sergei Prokofiev's *The Gambler*

POINTS

COMBINED POINTS

SING IT TO ME

How many of these great opera singers have you heard?

* Roberto Alagna
* Cecilia Bartoli
* Olga Borodina
* Annette Dasch
* Plácido Domingo
* Dmitri Hvorostovsky
* Bryn Terfel
* Anne Sofie von Otter

POINTS

OPERA FANATICS ONLY

Have you ever:

* Traveled to another city just to attend an opera?
* Worn formal clothes to an opera on opening night?
* Listened to a complete recording of the opera prior to attending?
* Read the libretto prior to attending?

POINTS

VOICES FROM THE PAST

Do you own any recordings by the following great opera singers?

* Maria Callas
* Enrico Caruso
* Kirsten Flagstad
* Birgit Nilsson
* Luciano Pavarotti
* Joan Sutherland

POINTS

COMBINED POINTS

WHAT A LAUGH

While most of the great operas are tragedies, comic operas are also part of the popular repertoire. Are you familiar with the following?

* Mozart's *Le Nozze di Figaro* (*The Marriage of Figaro*)
* Verdi's *Falstaff*
* Rossini's *The Barber of Seville*
* Wagner's *Die Meistersinger von Nürnberg* (*The Mastersingers of Nuremberg*)

POINTS

TAKES THE PRIZE

How many of these Pulitzer Prize–winning operas are you familiar with?

* *Madame White Snake* by Zhou Long
* *Life Is a Dream* by Lewis Spratlan
* *The Crucible* by Robert Ward
* *Vanessa* by Samuel Barber
* *The Saint of Bleecker Street* by Gian Carlo Menotti

POINTS

KIND OF TRUE

How many of these landmark jazz albums do you own?

* *Kind of Blue* by Miles Davis
* *Afro-Cuban Jazz Moods* by Dizzy Gillespie
* *Explorations* by Bill Evans
* *Chet Baker Sings* by Chet Baker
* *Jazz at Massey Hall* by Charlie Parker
* *A Love Supreme* by John Coltrane
* *Somethin' Else* by Julian "Cannonball" Adderley
* *Ellington at Newport* by Duke Ellington

POINTS

COMBINED POINTS

PASS THE BATON

Can you match these symphony orchestras with their conductors?

A. New York Philharmonic
B. Chicago Symphony Orchestra
C. Berlin Philharmonic
D. London Symphony Orchestra
E. Royal Concertgebouw Orchestra

1. Sir Simon Rattle
2. Alan Gilbert
3. Mariss Jansons
4. Riccardo Muti
5. Valery Gergiev

ANSWER: A, 2; B, 4; C, 1; D, 5; E, 3

POINTS

THE MUSIC OF DEATH

Which of the following funeral marches by famous composers have you heard?

* *Siegfried's Funeral March*, by Richard Wagner
* The second movement of *Symphony No. 3*, by Ludwig van Beethoven
* *The Funeral March for the Final Scene of Hamlet*, by Hector Berlioz
* *Funeral March of a Marionette*, by Charles Gounod

POINTS

NEW AND IMPROVED

Can you name the composers of these twentieth-century works?

1. *An American in Paris*
2. *Einstein on the Beach*
3. *The Firebird*
4. *Sonatas and Interludes*

ANSWER:

1. George Gershwin
2. Philip Glass
3. Igor Stravinsky
4. John Cage

POINTS

COMBINED POINTS

TURN IT UP

How many of these dynamics are you familiar with?

* Pianissimo – *pp* – very soft
* Piano – *p* – soft
* Mezzo piano – *mp* – moderately soft
* Mezzo forte – *mf* – moderately loud
* Forte – *f* – loud
* Fortissimo – *ff* – very loud

POINTS

MELODIOUS SOUNDS

Do you know these types of musical textures?

* Homophony—consists of a melody with an accompanying chordal harmony
* Polyphony—consists of two or more melodies
* Monophony—a texture that has one melody with no accompanying harmony

POINTS

CUE THE ORCHESTRA

Did you know these facts about symphonies?

* A symphony is typically composed of four movements
* These include an opening sonata or allegro, a slow movement such as adagio, a minuet with trio, and finally an allegro, rondo, or sonata
* Haydn wrote more than 108 symphonies
* Beethoven gave the symphony a tremendous boost in popularity
* The Berlioz symphony _____ has five movements

ANSWER: *Symphonie Fantastique*

POINTS

COMBINED POINTS

SCORING YOURSELF: MUSIC

Based on your responses to the checklists in the preceding section, use the rating system below to determine how you stand as a musical intellectual.

0–12: You undoubtedly have an ear of tin.

13–25: Keep your day job.

26–38: You may comfortably associate with musicians.

39–51: You could serenade the gods.

Chapter 4

History and Philosophy

The checklists in the History and Philosophy section are highly selective but broadly based. You'll be asked to identify events from the founding of this country to the greatest wars, and philosophers from Socrates to the existentialists.

Give yourself one point if you correctly identify all the elements in a checklist or answer the question. At the end of the section you'll have the opportunity to rate how intellectual you are on these subjects.

CHANGING OF THE GUARDS

The decline of the Roman Empire in A.D. 476 signaled the start of the Middle Ages. Are you familiar with these facts?

* Christianity dominated European civilization and thinking at this time
* There was little tolerance for the skeptical philosophies of the Greeks
* St. Augustine (early fifth century) was the first significant Christian philosopher
* He reasoned that understanding followed from faith
* Augustine also believed that the universe was ordered by a single spiritual entity

POINTS

MIDDLE-AGED THINKING

Learning and literacy advanced slowly for the next thousand years with a few notable events. Are you familiar with these?

* Learning was centered in the church and the clergy
* Scholasticism, a school of Christian thought that attempts to resolve questions of faith and reason, came into being around the year 1100
* The University of Oxford was founded in the early twelfth century
* St. Thomas Aquinas wrote a complete Christian theology
* He used Aristotelian principles to construct five arguments proving God's existence

POINTS

A RENAISSANCE IN PHILOSOPHY

Do you know these events that distinguished Renaissance thinking?

* The influence of Christian philosophy waned as printed texts became available
* Protestant reformers further diminished the church's power in the sixteenth century
* In the seventeenth century, Sir Francis Bacon espoused empiricism
* Empiricism, stressing experience and observation, paved the way for scientific methods

POINTS

COMBINED POINTS

SEEING IS BELIEVING

Which of these important historical sites have you visited?

* Bunker Hill, Boston
* Gettysburg, Pennsylvania
* Arlington Cemetery
* Mount Vernon

POINTS

BEFORE SOCRATES

As early as the seventh century B.C., Greeks had the leisure and willingness to consider the meaning of their existence. Are you aware of these early thinkers?

* Thales tried to provide rational explanations for natural phenomena
* Anaximander was a student of Thales but believed the universe's source was not matter
* Anaximenes believed that air was the primordial element
* All three explained the universe through what kind of causes?

ANSWER: These three thinkers posited natural rather than divine causes to explain the universe

POINTS

THE START OF SOMETHING BIG

The Renaissance came about due in large part to three inventions. Do you know what they are?

* Gunpowder—brought the destruction of the feudal order
* Block printing from movable type—propagated knowledge and secularized learning
* The compass—increased the safety of sea voyages that opened up the Western Hemisphere

POINTS

COMBINED POINTS

AN IMPORTANT DOCUMENT

The Constitution forms our governmental structure and provides fundamental protections for U.S. citizens. Did you know:

* The Constitution required the addition of ten amendments prior to ratification
* The Constitution was not ratified until 1789
* Since that time, seventeen amendments have been added
* The fourteenth amendment protects rights by defining "due process of law"

POINTS

SOPHISTS' CHOICE

The Sophists, or teachers, became active in Greece in the fifth century B.C. Did you know the following about this period?

* Expanding knowledge made it difficult for Greeks to keep up with developments
* Educating the young was compromised
* Sophists traveled between Greek cities and charged for their services
* They taught public speaking and argument to use in debate
* Their teaching contributed significantly to the development of oratory

POINTS

AN EARLY THEORY OF RELATIVITY

Protagoras was one of the first and most well known of the Sophists. Are you aware of his contributions?

* Protagoras taught as a Sophist for more than forty years, acquiring great wealth
* Plato named one of his dialogues after him
* Protagoras observed: "Man is the measure of all things" or truth is relative
* An agnostic, he was banished from Athens and his books were burned

POINTS

COMBINED POINTS

THE ROAD TO CIVIL WAR

The events leading to the American Civil War took place over centuries. How many of the following facts are you aware of?

* Twenty African men were brought to Jamestown, Virginia, as indentured servants in 1619
* Within fifty years, thousands of Africans had been sold as slaves in the American colonies
* By 1750, slavery was legal in all colonies
* Agricultural activities in the South became dependent on slave labor
* Labor-intensive crops such as cotton and tobacco were predominant

POINTS

SLAVERY IN THE UNITED STATES

How much of the history of slavery are you aware of?

* Until the early nineteenth century, slavery was legal in the North
* The North's soil and climate would not support large plantations, however
* In July 1787, Congress passed the Northwest Ordinance outlawing slavery in new states
* As a result, states in the Midwest did not allow slavery

POINTS

AMBIGUITY

The institution of slavery caused heated feelings on both sides of the issue. Did you know the following?

* Southern delegates to the 1787 Constitutional Convention wanted recognition of slavery
* Southern states threatened to withhold support of the Constitution if it contained antislavery measures
* Compromises permitted slaves to be counted for representation and taxation
* The Constitution also called for the return of escaped slaves
* However, a ban on the slave trade—within twenty years—was included

POINTS

COMBINED POINTS

MALICE TOWARD ALL

Tensions between advocates and opponents of slavery increased over time. Are you aware of the following events?

* In 1820, Congress argued over whether Missouri would be admitted as a slave state
* Speaker of the House Henry Clay, of Kentucky, worked out a compromise
* The Missouri Compromise admitted Maine as a free state and Missouri as a slave state
* Slavery was also banned in the remaining Louisiana Territory above a certain parallel
* Thomas Jefferson referred to the dispute as "the death knell of the Union"

POINTS

NO COMPROMISE

Drastic measures seemed inevitable as both sides became entrenched. Did you know the following?

* South Carolina politicians began talking about states' rights in 1828
* Nat Turner led a slave revolt in Virginia in 1831
* The South's dissent over tariffs was brought under control by President Jackson in 1832
* Southerners attempted to portray slavery as beneficial for the nearly 4 million slaves
* Northern abolitionists painted the institution as immoral

POINTS

CONSTRICTIONS ON
WESTWARD EXPANSION

The issue of slavery dominated most events at this time. Were you aware of the following?

* The war with Mexico in 1846, fought over Texas, became tinged by slavery issues
* Some Northerners opposed the war, not wanting Texas to be admitted as a slave state
* A Pennsylvania congressman introduced the Wilmot Proviso in 1846
* The Wilmot Proviso would have banned slavery in the new territory, but was not passed
* Some northern Democrats left the party to form the Free Soil Party

POINTS

COMBINED POINTS

DESPERATE MEASURES

In an attempt to maintain Union stability, Congress passed the Compromise of 1850. Its provisions included all but which of the following?

A. Admitted California to the Union as a free state
B. Allowed New Mexico and Utah to decide on slavery by popular vote
C. Banned the internal slave trade from Washington, D.C.
D. Established a special committee of senators to debate the issues
E. Enforced the Fugitive Slave Law, requiring all citizens to return escaped slaves

ANSWER: D

POINTS

THE FINAL HOURS

The decade before the Civil War was eventful. Do you know about the following events?

* Harriet Beecher Stowe's *Uncle Tom's Cabin* (1852) created an uproar
* Congress passed the Kansas-Nebraska Act (1854) repealing the Missouri Compromise
* The act permitted the new territories to decide about slavery by popular vote
* The Supreme Court ruled against fugitive slave Dred Scott in 1857

* John Brown and militant abolitionists attacked a Virginia armory in 1859
* A new Republican Party was formed in opposition to slavery, led by

_____

ANSWER: Abraham Lincoln

POINTS

READING MATTER

Can you match the authors with their books about the Civil War?

A. Charles Royster

B. Doris Kearns Goodwin

C. Eric Foner

D. David W. Blight

E. Drew Gilpin Faust

1. _Team of Rivals: The Political Genius of Abraham Lincoln_

2. _The Fiery Trial: Abraham Lincoln and American Slavery_

3. _Race and Reunion: The Civil War in American Memory_

4. _This Republic of Suffering: Death and the American Civil War_

5. _The Destructive War: William Tecumseh Sherman, Stonewall Jackson, and the Americans_

ANSWER: A, 5; B, 1; C, 2; D, 3; E, 4

POINTS

COMBINED POINTS

SOCRATES

Socrates is considered the most important philosopher in the history of Western thought. Do you know this about him?

* We have none of his writings
* Socrates believed that ethics should be proven; truth is not relative
* He frequently debated his ideas in public places
* His pupil, Plato, wrote down his ideas in twenty-four dialogues
* Socrates took his own life by _____

ANSWER: drinking hemlock

POINTS

PLATO

Plato was a pupil and disciple of Socrates. How many of these facts about Plato do you know?

* Plato was just twenty-nine when Socrates died
* His most influential works were dialogues featuring Socrates
* In *Phaedo*, he introduces the idea of "forms," abstract ideas like beauty and justice
* *Symposium* discusses love of all kinds
* *The Republic* is his dialogue about a community based on justice

POINTS

ARISTOTLE

Aristotle was a pupil in Plato's Academy for twenty years. Did you know this about him?

* He disagreed with Plato's theory of forms as fixed and absolute
* He suggested that those concepts meant different things to different people
* Our word "peripatetic" derives from the Academy students' habit of walking about
* His writings were lost and not studied in the West until the early Middle Ages
* Aristotle tutored Alexander the Great

POINTS

COMBINED POINTS

SETTING THE STAGE FOR WORLD WAR

The world was unstable at the beginning of the twentieth century and events were unfolding quickly. How many of the following events are you aware of?

* The Boer War (1899–1902) was an uprising in South Africa against British rule
* Japan revealed its imperialistic tendencies when it defeated Russia in a brief war in 1905
* Mounting tensions caused Britain to form an alliance with France and Russia—the Allies
* Germany aligned with Austria-Hungary and the Ottoman Empire—the Central Powers

POINTS

THE WAR TO END ALL WARS

The assassination of the heir to the throne of Austria-Hungary was the spark needed to bring Europe, Britain, and Russia into World War I. Can you pick out the facts from the list below?

A. In the East, the Central Powers devastated Russian forces in 1914
B. The Central Powers were able to advance and occupy Paris at the beginning of the war
C. Greater firepower was not matched by improvements in fighting strategy
D. The Russian Revolution of 1917 brought Lenin to power
E. Russia signed a truce with Germany and fighting increased in the West

ANSWER: Statements A, C, D, and E are true. B is not.

POINTS

A NEW HOPE

World War I might have ended differently if the United States had not gotten involved. Are you aware of these events?

* Attacks on American ships caused the United States to declare war on Germany in April 1917
* American troops landed in France in June 1917 and halted German offensives in 1918
* Allied forces, with American reinforcements, launched a major offensive in September 1918
* Germany saw the hopelessness of its efforts in the field and experienced unrest at home
* Germany asked for peace terms and an armistice was signed in November 1918

POINTS

COMBINED POINTS

FORGIVENESS AND REVENGE

In 1919, President Woodrow Wilson attended a peace conference in Paris. Do you know these results of the First World War?

* Wilson wished to create a League of Nations
* He also wanted to forgive the Central Powers's financial responsibility
* French and British leaders wanted to treat Germany as a conquered nation
* The Treaty of Versailles called for reparations, the returning of land, and demilitarization
* Humiliated Germans began to rally around Adolf Hitler, who called for vengeance

POINTS

A PERSONAL POINT OF VIEW

How many of the important sites of World War I have you seen in person?

* Verdun, France
* Canadian War Memorial at Vimy Ridge, France
* Thiepval Monument and Museum, Thiepval, France
* Museum of the Great War, Péronne, France

POINTS

BETWEEN THE COVERS

Can you identify the authors of these books on World War I?

A. *The First World War*
B. *The First World War*
C. *Europe's Last Summer*
D. *Dreadnought*
E. *The Guns of August*

1. Robert K. Massie
2. John Keegan
3. Hew Strachan
4. Barbara Wertheim Tuchman
5. David Fromkin

ANSWER: A, 2; B, 3; C, 5; D, 1; E, 4

POINTS

COMBINED POINTS

SCHOOLS OF THOUGHT

Athens was the leading center of philosophic thought during the Hellenistic period (323–31 B.C.). Do you know what the famous schools of philosophy were at that time?

* Plato's Academy was established in beginning of the fourth century B.C.
* Aristotle's Peripatos was created in the second half of that century
* The Stoic school was started by Zeno of Citium (around 300 B.C.)
* The Kepos school was developed by Epicurus at about the same time
* The Skeptics were led by Pyrrho of Elis

POINTS

COMPETING VISIONS

Having invented the idea of philosophy, the Greeks put a lot of effort into it. Did you know the following?

* Our word "philosophy" comes from the Greek *philosophos*, "love of wisdom"
* The Skeptics questioned the basis of knowledge and denied its possibility
* The Epicureans believed only in the physical world and attempted to eliminate pain
* The Stoics tried to understand and live by the principles that control the world

POINTS

STEADFAST

Stoic thinking produced many lasting effects. How many of the following facts do you know?

* Stoic indifference showed an acceptance of the order of things
* Romans who adopted Stoicism included Seneca, Epictetus, and Emperor Marcus Aurelius
* Stoicism was the source for the belief in the fundamental equality of all people
* Stoics also believed in natural rights for people
* Stoics admired Socrates for his steadfast belief in universal principles

POINTS

COMBINED POINTS

A FAILED VISION

Less than twenty years separated two world wars. How many of these events leading up to World War II are you aware of?

* The League of Nations was created but the U.S. Senate refused to ratify the treaty
* Germany was crushed by economic depression and political upheaval in the 1920s
* Hitler formed the Nazi party and became chancellor in 1933 to restore German dignity
* In Italy, Benito Mussolini established a totalitarian state
* Japan became a military power and invaded China in 1937

POINTS

THE SECOND COMING

Germany's desire to avenge itself was ignored until it was too late. Did you know these facts about World War II?

* Hitler rebuilt Germany's armed forces and invaded Austria in 1938
* Britain and France capitulated to Germany's demand to annex Czechoslovakia
* At home, Hitler instituted policies that led to the Holocaust, which resulted in the death of 6 million Jews
* In 1939, Germany invaded Poland, and Britain and France declared war
* France fell and Hitler controlled most of Europe by _____

* Germany attacked the Soviet Union in 1941 in violation of their secret pact
* America remained neutral, although it supplied arms to Britain's war with Germany

ANSWER: June 1939

POINTS

OFF TO WAR

Once again the United States had to respond to military aggression. Were you aware of the following?

* America criticized Japan's aggressive behavior; Japan attacked the United States in 1941
* America declared war on Japan; Japan's allies Germany and Italy declared war on the United States
* Though concentrating efforts in Europe, America scored big victories against Japan
* Germany suffered a big defeat against the Soviet Union in 1943
* June 1944 saw the Allied landing and another year of fighting before victory in Europe
* The atomic bombing of two Japanese cities forced Japan to surrender in August 1945

POINTS

COMBINED POINTS

LESSONS LEARNED

Between 60 and 70 million people, mostly civilians, died in World War II. Are you aware of these other consequences of the war?

* Nearly 300,000 American servicemen were killed in the war
* There were an estimated 21 million war refugees in Europe
* Fifty-one nations, including the United States, were inspired to found the United Nations
* The Cold War between the United States and the Soviet Union started over disagreement about occupation of Eastern Europe
* Mistrust grew from perceived threats of atomic power

POINTS

HALLOWED GROUND

How many of these World War II memorials have you visited?

* USS Arizona Memorial, Pearl Harbor, Hawaii
* Hiroshima Peace Park, Hiroshima, Japan
* Normandy American Cemetery and Memorial, Normandy, France
* Volgograd State Panoramic Museum (Battle of Stalingrad), Volgograd, Russia
* Auschwitz Museum and Memorial, Oswiecim, Poland
* United States Holocaust Memorial Museum, Washington, D.C.

POINTS

GETTING A PERSPECTIVE

How many of these World War II histories have you read?

* *Crusade in Europe* by Dwight Eisenhower
* *A World at Arms* by Gerhard Weinberg
* *Why the Allies Won* by Richard Overy
* *The Second World War* by John Keegan
* *The Origins of the Second World War* by A. J. P. Taylor
* *The Rise and Fall of the Third Reich* by William Shirer
* *Hitler: A Study in Tyranny* by Alan Bullock

POINTS

COMBINED POINTS

THE ANCHORS OF BELIEF

Do you know the following about the thinking of Confucius?

* Confucius sought to understand the present by concentrating on the past
* He believed that living a ritualized life would give the past meaning
* His love of the past came from his desire to understand the longevity of certain institutions
* Reverence for ancestors and mourning ceremonies, for example, had lasted for centuries
* Confucius thought of himself as a conservationist of cultural values and social norms

POINTS

FIVE CORE IDEAS

Confucianism is a way of thinking and living that the Chinese people have followed for more than 2,000 years. Can you match the core ideas of Confucianism with their names?

A. *ren*

B. *li*

C. *zhong*

D. *shu*

E. *xiao*

1. reciprocity

2. humaneness or benevolence

3. ritual norms

4. filial piety

5. loyalty to one's true nature

ANSWER: A, 2; B, 3; C, 5; D, 1; E, 4

POINTS

THE GREAT MASTER K'UNG

Confucius was the best known and most influential thinker in Chinese history. Do you know these facts about Confucius?

* Confucius was born in 551 B.C.
* He served in minor government positions before starting his teaching career in his thirties
* He is known as the first teacher in China who wanted to make education widely available
* He was also one of the first to establish teaching as a vocation
* When he died in 479 B.C., how many people claimed to be his followers? (A) 100, (B) 1,000, (C) 3,000, or (D) 10,000

ANSWER: C

POINTS

COMBINED POINTS

GREAT BEGINNINGS

Mencius was a contemporary of Plato and interpreter of Confucius. Do you know his four beginnings of human nature?

* The feeling of commiseration is the beginning of humanity
* The feeling of shame and dislike is the beginning of righteousness
* The feeling of deference and compliance is the beginning of propriety
* The feeling of right or wrong is the beginning of wisdom

POINTS

BRINKSMANSHIP

The Cold War shaped the American worldview for forty years. Do you know these facts about the beginning of this period?

* The term "Cold War" was coined by the author George Orwell in 1945
* Winston Churchill first used the term "Iron Curtain" to describe the Western/Soviet divide
* Both Korea and Germany (and Berlin) were divided into democratic and communist zones
* The Truman Doctrine, a policy opposing the spread of communism, was announced in 1947

POINTS

RAMPING UP

Opposition and Cold War tensions increased quickly. Are you aware of these developments?

* The Soviets created a blockade around Berlin in 1948, which was overcome by an airlift
* The United States entered into the North Atlantic Treaty Organization with its European allies in 1949
* The Soviet bloc responded to the anti-Soviet NATO in 1955 with the Warsaw Pact
* The Soviet Union exploded its first atomic bomb in 1949

POINTS

COMBINED POINTS

THE CHINA SYNDROME

Communism was growing in eastern Asia in the middle of the twentieth century. Did you know the following?

* Chinese communists led by Mao Zedong drove out the pro-West nationalists in 1949
* The Soviet-backed communist government of North Korea invaded South Korea in 1950
* American-led U.N forces came to the aid of South Korea
* The Korean War lasted until 1953, ending without a clear outcome

POINTS

COMMUNISTS EVERYWHERE

Cold War tensions created unease and fear in the American public. Do you know these manifestations of that fear?

* In 1952, Republicans were able to win the White House for the first time since 1928
* Dwight Eisenhower, a war hero, was elected president
* Wisconsin Sen. Joseph McCarthy became America's leading anti-communist
* McCarthy claimed to have knowledge of Soviet agents and made vigorous accusations
* His influence faded in 1953 when he claimed the U.S. Army was harboring communists

POINTS

MUTUALLY ASSURED DESTRUCTION

The Cold War resulted in an arms race between the West and the Soviet Union, which in turn increased tensions. Are you aware of these events?

* In 1961, East Germany started construction of the Berlin Wall to stop defections
* In 1962, the Soviet Union began to secretly install missiles in Cuba
* The resulting Cuban Missile Crisis brought the two powers to the brink of war
* A U.S. naval blockade of Cuba brought about the withdrawal of the missiles
* The two powers signed a treaty in 1963 banning aboveground testing of nuclear weapons

POINTS

COMBINED POINTS

MAINTAINING A BALANCE

Relations between East and West were complicated as well as tense through the 1970s. Did you know the following?

* Soviets sent troops to protect their interests in Hungary, Czechoslovakia, and Afghanistan
* The United States helped overthrow a leftist government in Guatemala and supported the unsuccessful Bay of Pigs invasion into Cuba
* The Vietnam War was a costly and unsuccessful attempt to halt communism's spread

POINTS

DESCARTES

René Descartes was the dominant thinker in the last half of the seventeenth century. Do you know the following about him?

* Descartes combined classical thinking with the scientific outlook of his age
* He is considered the precursor to the modern spirit of philosophy
* In *Principles of Philosophy* (1644) he defined philosophy as "the study of wisdom"
* Descartes was a mathematician and scientist and based his ideas on certainty
* "I think, therefore I am" was his conclusion

POINTS

HOBBES WITHOUT CALVIN

Thomas Hobbes was a seventeenth-century English scholar deeply interested in government. How many of the following facts do you know about him?

* Hobbes knew both Francis Bacon and Galileo
* He had a strong interest in the philosophical method as well as matter in motion
* He traveled extensively, researching the functioning of government
* He advanced the idea of a "social contract" between rulers and the ruled
* Hobbes felt people were wicked and that life was "nasty, brutish, and short"

POINTS

COMBINED POINTS

ENLIGHTEN ME

The intellectual movement in Europe in the seventeenth and eighteenth centuries is referred to as the Enlightenment. Did you know the following?

* Thought centered on political philosophy, the role of government, and people
* John Locke developed modern ideas of identity and self—that we are born without innate ideas
* Locke also advanced the concept of "government with the consent of the governed"
* The first encyclopedia based on rational values of the Enlightenment was published
* The French crown attempted to censor its liberal ideas and criticisms of government
* Voltaire observed: "If God did not exist, he would have to be invented"

POINTS

ENLIGHTENED THINKER

Jean-Jacques Rousseau contributed significantly to the Enlightenment. How many of the following facts are you aware?

* Rousseau was brilliant but extremely paranoid and mentally unbalanced
* He believed humans were born innocent in contradiction to the Christian belief of original sin

* His *The Social Contract* (1762) claims freedom is the ultimate goal of society
* Rousseau's ideas about education in his novel *Emile* (1762) are still influential

POINTS [　　　]

ENLIGHTENED THINKER TOO

Immanuel Kant was one of the Enlightenment's foremost thinkers. Did you know:

* Kant published *Critique of Pure Reason* in 1781
* He argued that certain ideas (God, freedom) could be believed but not experienced
* He believed that the individual could find freedom in living by universal moral principles
* His moral philosophy influenced such intellectuals as Nietzsche and Freud

POINTS [　　　]

COMBINED POINTS [　　　]

HONORING THE FALLEN

How many of these national war memorials have you visited in person?

* World War I Memorial
* National World War II Memorial
* Korean War Veterans Memorial
* Vietnam Veterans Memorial

POINTS

RECITE YOUR RHETORIC

From which of these famous American speeches can you quote, verbatim:

* Lincoln's Gettysburg Address
* JFK's inaugural address
* FDR's Pearl Harbor address to the nation
* Emerson's "The American Scholar" speech
* Dr. Martin Luther King Jr.'s last speech

POINTS

A BUSY TIME

Philosophy in the nineteenth century was affected by major changes. Which of the following was *not* a factor?

A. The Romantic Movement was a literary revolt against reason
B. The Industrial Revolution prompted calls for social reform
C. The American Civil War caused philosophers to question race identity
D. Revolutions in Europe in mid-century sparked class consciousness
E. Darwin's work in evolution increased biological science knowledge

ANSWER: C

POINTS

COMBINED POINTS

NOT JUST GOOD, IDEAL

The first part of the nineteenth century was dominated by the German philosophy of absolute idealism. Do you know its proponents and concepts?

* Idealism was influenced by Romanticism and by a new alliance with religion
* It was based on understanding of the self and the spiritual world
* Johann Fichte wrote that the moral will is the chief characteristic of the self
* Georg Wilhelm Friedrich Hegel believed that reason changes and has a cultural dimension
* Hegel said that struggle is the essence of spiritual existence

POINTS

A BETTER IDEA

In the middle of the nineteenth century, new thinkers came to prominence and new philosophies arose. Did you know that:

* In France, Auguste Comte published his antireligious philosophy of positivism
* Positivism accepted only knowledge derived through accepted scientific methods
* In England, John Stuart Mill released *A System of Logic*
* Mill espoused scientific principles and advocated political liberalism
* The German Karl Marx published *The Communist Manifesto* in 1848
* Marx exposed the struggle of the worker and advocated violent overthrow of the social order

POINTS

COMBINED POINTS

GOING FROM BAD TO WORSE

Do you know these nineteenth-century irrationalist philosophers?

* Søren Kierkegaard preached concrete action and emotion as opposed to mere thought
* Arthur Schopenhauer said that science could not penetrate the real world
* Friedrich Nietzsche felt the philosopher should destroy old values and create new ideals
* These three philosophers viewed the human mind as dark and obscure

POINTS

PHILOSOPHY TODAY

Philosophy in the twentieth century has become a profession. Are you aware that:

* Most philosophers today are part of academia
* Philosophers deal with specialized issues and employ a technical nomenclature
* Schools of thought are distinctly defined and the nature of philosophy is contested
* English-speaking philosophers tend toward logical analysis
* European philosophers follow a speculative and historical tradition

POINTS

LET'S THINK ABOUT THIS

In keeping with their professionalism, twentieth-century philosophers developed an analytic method. Did you know the following?

* Analytic philosophy approaches problems by first clarifying the issue
* Practitioners have created symbolic language and examined speech to help achieve clarity
* The creation of symbolic logic provided formal techniques for some philosophers
* Much of the century's analysis was focused on meaning and reference in language

POINTS

COMBINED POINTS

GETTING SMALL

The mathematician and philosopher Bertrand Russell developed the theory of logical atomism at the beginning of the twentieth century. Do you know these facts about it?

* Mathematical logic could reveal the basic structure of reality hidden in language
* The world is made up of simple, or "atomic" facts, which are made of objects
* These atomic facts are mind-independent features of reality
* Propositions of logic refer to atomic facts
* There is a connection between languages and the structure of the real world

POINTS

EXISTENTIALISM

Existentialism was a twentieth-century philosophy that approached mainstream acceptance. Did you know the following?

* The German Karl Jaspers was an existentialist philosopher
* Jaspers believed that an individual realizes his humanity by confronting extremes
* The French philosopher Jean-Paul Sartre is the best-known existentialist
* Sartre believed that the essence of "being" could be found in liberty
* He felt that a person should overcome limitations through acts of conscious decision
* His companion Simone de Beauvoir expressed existential thought in feminist terms

POINTS

COMBINED POINTS

SCORING YOURSELF:
HISTORY AND PHILOSOPHY

Based on your responses to the checklists in the preceding section, use the rating system below to determine how you stand as an intellectual in the fields of history and philosophy.

0–15: It's apparent that you see little value in history.

16–30: You have enough knowledge of history and philosophy to safely appear in public.

31–45: Your knowledge is commendable.

46–61: You have a comprehensive understanding of history and philosophy.

Chapter 5

Politics

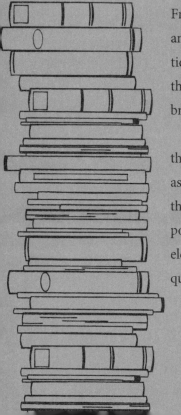

From the origins of political science as an academic discipline to the latest elections, the Politics checklists will give you the opportunity to demonstrate your broad understanding of this topic.

At the end of the section you'll have the opportunity to rate your standing as a political intellectual. As you read through the checklists, give yourself one point if you correctly identify all the elements in a checklist or answer the question.

POLI SCI 101

Political science as an academic discipline and study didn't begin until the nineteenth century, although its roots run much earlier. Did you know these facts about the discipline?

* Domestic politics—elections and government—is the most common field of study
* Comparative politics analyzes politics within and between countries
* International relations considers such subjects as war and foreign policy
* Political theory includes classical and contemporary political philosophy
* Public administration studies the role of bureaucracies

POINTS

A MAN WITH A PLAN

A number of early thinkers analyzed politics, but Aristotle is considered the founder of political science. Did you know the following about his political thought?

* Aristotle's students gathered information about the Greek city-states
* Aristotle used this information to create his typology of political systems
* He classified political systems by the number of persons ruling and by legitimacy
* He considered legitimate systems as those operated in the interests of the citizens

* Legitimate systems included monarchy, aristocracy, and polity (rule by the many)
* He noted that polities function best with a large middle class

POINTS

ROMAN IDEAS

Were you aware of these changes in political thought in early Roman times?

* Aristotle's classification system was still useful in understanding political systems
* He and Plato both considered society and political system as a single concept
* After the death of Alexander the Great, new political forms were created
* Society and political systems became distinct entities
* The Stoics and others asserted a natural law and the worth of all human beings

POINTS

COMBINED POINTS

POLITICS IS SAVED

The rise of Christianity inspired a religious view of political systems. Did you know the following?

* St. Augustine (ca. 400) noted that the "heavenly city" is more important than the earthly
* St. Thomas Aquinas (ca. 1250) translated Aristotle's *Politics*, giving it a moral purpose
* Aquinas argued that government could be used for good and human spiritual improvement
* Italian poet and philosopher Dante advocated a single world government

POINTS

NOT SO FAST

Another Italian author, Niccolò Machiavelli (1469–1527), is considered the first modern political scientist. Are you aware of the following facts about him?

* His work *The Prince* (1532) offers unethical advice to princes who wish to acquire power
* His philosophy completely secularizes politics
* He reasoned that ruthless power without moral constraint was necessary to save Italy
* Machiavelli introduced the modern concept of the use of power as pivotal in politics

POINTS

THOUGHTFUL THOUGHTS

The English philosopher Thomas Hobbes, having witnessed civil war, expressed his political views in the seventeenth century. Did you know the following?

* His major work in 1651, _____, advances the idea of a social contract
* The social contract is an expressed or indefinite agreement between ruler and ruled
* The contract is secular in nature
* It is a natural outgrowth of the human need for security

ANSWER: *Leviathan*

POINTS

COMBINED POINTS

SOUND IDEAS

The English philosopher John Locke was witness to a civil war. Do you know the following about his political work?

* His *Two Treatises of Government* (1690) reinforced the idea of social contracts
* He argued that people form governments to preserve certain inalienable natural rights
* These rights include "life, liberty, and property"
* He also claimed that a government failing in this responsibility may be overthrown
* These ideas are reanimated in the United States's Declaration of Independence

POINTS

BETTER IDEAS

In the eighteenth century, two more English philosophers brought political thought further. Are you aware of the following facts?

* The Scotsman Adam Smith is considered the founder of economic liberalism
* He argued that the role of government should be strictly limited
* His seminal work, published in 1776, was _____
* Edmund Burke (1729–97) believed that established values and institutions were essential

* He introduced the idea that political systems grow and change over time

ANSWER: *An Inquiry into the Nature and Causes of the Wealth of Nations*

POINTS

REFINEMENTS

The nineteenth century brought further developments in political science. Did you know the following?

* Growth of the natural sciences stimulated interest in a new social science
* French thinkers suggested that societal ideas could be built on objective evidence
* Alexis de Tocqueville analyzed American democracy in the 1830s
* He found a democracy functioning on the pillars of liberty and equality
* By contrast, Marx and Engels argued for an economic theory of the state
* They saw the working class establishing socialism as a just government

POINTS

COMBINED POINTS

MORE THAN JUST AN ART

Political science had accumulated enough study and analysis to become a discipline. Did you know about these events that occurred at the dawn of the twentieth century?

* The first separate school of political science was established in France in 1872
* Columbia University established political science as a separate discipline in 1880
* Woodrow Wilson, president during World War I, was an early scholar of political science
* He and others were influenced by intellectual developments such as evolution
* American political science transformed to the study of social facts

POINTS

CONTINUING DEBATES

Aside from the question concerning the purpose of political science—to analyze political events or to promote better political systems—the discipline faces numerous debates. Are you aware of these issues?

* Structuralists argue that the world's organization determines politics
* Cultural theorists claim values, opinions, and psychology are more important
* Some scientists believe that elites pursue their own goals and manipulate public opinion
* Another theory holds that elites are directed by citizen preferences
* Political science as a discipline is considered to have a major failing. What is it?

ANSWER: An important failing is political science's inability to predict events

POINTS

COMBINED POINTS

LOTS OF CHOICES

Besides the Democratic and Republican nominees, other candidates ran for president in the 2008 election. Can you identify them and their parties?

A. Pastor and talk show host Chuck Baldwin

B. Georgia congresswoman Cynthia McKinney

C. Former representative Bob Barr

D. Activist Brian Moore

E. Attorney and activist Ralph Nader

1. Green Party

2. Independent campaign

3. Constitution Party

4. Libertarian Party

5. Socialist Party USA

ANSWER: A, 3; B, 1; C, 4; D, 5; E, 2

POINTS

A FEW FIRSTS

The 2008 election was unique in several respects. Do you know what they are?

* It was the first time an African American was elected president
* It was the first time in which two current senators ran against each other
* It was the first election in fifty-six years in which neither an incumbent president nor a vice president ran
* It was the first time the Republican Party nominated a woman for vice president
* Barack Obama received the most votes for a presidential candidate in history

POINTS

CITIZENSHIP

In the most recent national or local elections in which an elected office was contested, did you:

* Attend a campaign event to listen to a candidate speak
* Attend an event held by the opposition candidate
* Attend a debate between candidates if one was held
* Vote

POINTS

COMBINED POINTS

THE INVOLVED CITIZEN

In order to exercise your rights as an American, have you ever done any of the following:

* Written to your congressional representative
* Worked for the campaign committee of a candidate for office you support
* Helped gather signatures for a petition for a political cause
* Convinced a friend or family member to vote in an election

POINTS

READING MATTER(S)

How many of the following politically oriented magazines do you read on a regular basis?

* *The American Spectator*
* *Foreign Policy*
* *The National Interest*
* *Harper's*
* *The New Republic*
* *The Atlantic*
* *The Economist*

POINTS [ ]

POWER TO THE PEOPLE

Which of the following twentieth-century revolutionaries did not follow the principles established by Karl Marx?

A. Vladimir Lenin
B. Dalai Lama
C. Mao Zedong
D. Ho Chi Minh
E. Fidel Castro

ANSWER: B

POINTS [ ]

COMBINED POINTS [ ]

COURT TIME

How many of these landmark decisions by the Supreme Court can you identify?

* *Plessy v. Ferguson* (1896) affirmed _____
* *West Virginia State Board of Education v. Barnette* (1943) ruled _____
* *Brown v. Board of Education of Topeka* (1954) overruled _____
* *Griswold v. Connecticut* (1965) established _____
* *Miranda v. Arizona* (1966) required _____
* *Roe v. Wade* (1973) ruled _____

ANSWER:

1. *Plessy v. Ferguson* affirmed the "separate but equal" segregation doctrine
2. *West Virginia State Board of Education v. Barnette* ruled that the First Amendment protected the "right of silence"
3. *Brown v. Board of Education of Topeka* overruled the "separate but equal" doctrine and integrated schools
4. *Griswold v. Connecticut* established a citizen's right to privacy
5. *Miranda v. Arizona* required suspects to be advised of their rights
6. *Roe v. Wade* ruled that abortion restrictions violated the right to privacy

POINTS

SPRINGTIME IN THE MIDDLE EAST

During the first few months of 2011, many countries in the Middle East experienced pro-democracy rebellions and protests, the so-called "Arab Spring." Can you name the countries that experienced these rebellions and protests?

ANSWER: In alphabetical order: Algeria, Bahrain, Egypt, Iran, Iraq, Jordan, Kuwait, Lebanon, Libya, Morocco, Palestine, Saudi Arabia, Syria, Tunisia, United Arab Emirates, Yemen

POINTS

THE BASICS

Can you match these classic books on political thought to their authors?

A. *The Cultural Contradictions of Capitalism*   1. Aleksandr Solzhenitsyn

B. *Main Currents of Marxism*   2. Daniel Bell

C. *Anarchy, State and Utopia*   3. Quentin Skinner

D. *The Foundations of Modern Political Thought*   4. Leszek Kolakowski

E. *The Gulag Archipelago*   5. Robert Nozick

ANSWER: A, 2; B, 4; C, 5; D, 3; E, 1

POINTS

COMBINED POINTS

WHAT OTHERS ARE SAYING

Have you read these recent important political books?

* *The Capitalist Revolution: Fifty Propositions About Prosperity, Equality and Liberty* by Peter Berger
* *Nations and Nationalism* by Ernest Gellner
* *The Rise and Fall of the Great Powers* by Paul Kennedy
* *Spheres of Justice* by Michael Walzer

POINTS

SOURCES OF POWER

Can you name what happens in each of these buildings, which serve as seats of government power?

1. U.S. Capitol
2. White House
3. Supreme Court
4. The Pentagon

ANSWER:

1. The U.S. Capitol holds the meeting chambers of the House of Representatives and the Senate.
2. The president and his family live and work in the White House.
3. The justices of the Supreme Court decide matters of law here.
4. The Department of Defense is headquartered at the Pentagon.

POINTS

REMEMBERING

How many of these sites honoring the contributions of important Americans have you seen?

* Woodrow Wilson House Museum
* African American Civil War Memorial
* Washington Monument
* Jefferson Memorial
* Lincoln Memorial

POINTS

COMBINED POINTS

A BIG JOB

Can you name the four main purposes of the United Nations?

* To keep peace throughout the world
* To develop friendly relations among nations
* To help nations work together to improve the lives of their people
* To be a center for harmonizing the actions of nations to achieve these goals

POINTS

ALL IN ONE BUILDING

Did you know the following about the United Nations?

* There are currently 192 member states
* All internationally recognized sovereign states are members, except Vatican City
* The UN has six official languages: Arabic, Chinese, English, French, Russian, and Spanish
* The International Court of Justice adjudicates disputes between states
* The International Criminal Court tries violators of international law

POINTS

LEADERSHIP

Can you name the last four Secretaries-General of the United Nations?

* Ban Ki-moon
* Kofi Annan
* Boutros Boutros-Ghali
* Javier Pérez de Cuéllar

POINTS

A TOUGH JOB

Can you name the last five United States Ambassadors to the United Nations?

* Susan Rice
* Zalmay Khalilzad
* Alejandro Daniel Wolff
* John R. Bolton
* Anne W. Patterson

POINTS

COMBINED POINTS

SOMEBODY'S GOT TO DO IT

In the following list, who was *not* a United States Ambassador to the United Nations?

A. John Danforth
B. Marlin Fitzwater
C. Richard Holbrooke
D. Bill Richardson
E. Madeleine Albright

ANSWER: B

POINTS

BIG GOALS

All United Nations member states have agreed to achieve the Millennium Development Goals by 2015. Can you name all of the goals?

* Eradicate extreme poverty and hunger
* Achieve universal primary education
* Promote gender equality and empower women
* Reduce child mortality rates, improve maternal health, combat diseases
* Ensure environmental sustainability
* Develop a global partnership for development

POINTS

A LONG LIST OF ACCOMPLISHMENTS

Do you know the following about the United Nations?

* It has more than 120,000 military, police, and civilians serving worldwide
* The UN is credited with having reduced conflict worldwide by 40 percent since the 1990s
* The UN has authorized sixty-four peacekeeping and observer missions over the past sixty years
* The UN has played a role in bringing about independence in more than eighty countries
* The United Nations and Kofi Annan won the 2001 Nobel Peace Prize

POINTS

COMBINED POINTS

A THINKING PRESIDENT

Did you know the following about the twenty-eighth president, Woodrow Wilson?

* Early in his career, he believed the United States should adopt a parliamentary system
* Wilson was president of Princeton University and governor of New Jersey
* A Progressive, he advocated change through government action
* He started the Federal Reserve System and Federal Trade Commission
* He instituted the federal income tax and the first antitrust legislation

POINTS

A VALIANT EFFORT

As president during the First World War, Woodrow Wilson had a significant influence on domestic and world politics. Were you aware of the following facts?

* Wilson attempted to keep America out of the war and refused to build up the U.S. Army
* The United States made a declaration of neutrality in 1914
* Wilson advocated entering the war in 1917 after German attacks on U.S. merchant ships
* His Fourteen Points of 1918 explained U.S. war aims and provided a framework for peace
* He suppressed opposition to the war with the Espionage Act and Sedition Act
* He received the 1919 Nobel Peace Prize but his League of Nations efforts failed

POINTS

COMBINED POINTS

LITTLE TO SAY

Calvin Coolidge was America's thirtieth president (1923–1929). Did you know these facts about him?

* He was a progressive Massachusetts state representative, voting for women's suffrage
* He was both lieutenant governor and governor of Massachusetts
* He received national attention for standing up to a Boston police strike
* He supported workers' rights and imposed economic controls as governor
* Later as president, he reduced taxes and federal government spending

POINTS

SPEAK UP

The policies of Calvin Coolidge's presidency were criticized as leading to the Great Depression. Did you know these facts about the years he was president?

* The economy was expanding rapidly during the "Roaring Twenties"
* Coolidge lowered taxes, and by 1927, only two percent of the population paid federal income tax
* Despite falling farm prices, Coolidge vetoed farm subsidies
* He spoke out in favor of civil rights of minorities, reducing the Ku Klux Klan's power
* Coolidge did not support _____ as his successor

ANSWER: Herbert Hoover

POINTS

COMBINED POINTS

START DIGGING

Herbert Hoover was America's thirty-first president (1929–1933). He oversaw and was defeated by the Great Depression. Did you know the following about Hoover?

* He earned a degree in geology and wrote a mining textbook
* He helped organize humanitarian relief efforts for European victims of World War I
* President Warren Harding appointed him Secretary of Commerce
* He began efforts to improve relations between business and government
* He promoted international trade and improved efficiency in industry

POINTS

FROM BAD TO WORSE

Herbert Hoover was elected president on the basis of his national reputation as secretary of commerce. Were you aware of the events of his administration?

* Hoover came into office advocating "voluntarism" rather than government intervention
* He believed that self-reliance was a key American value to be encouraged
* After the 1929 stock market crash, he initially asked for the cooperation of business
* He was unwilling to fund welfare programs for out-of-work Americans
* He used troops to forcibly remove jobless WWI veterans from Washington, D.C.
* He forced half a million Mexicans in the United States to leave the country
* Higher tariffs from the Smoot-Hawley Act spread the Depression worldwide

POINTS

COMBINED POINTS

HARD TIMES

Franklin D. Roosevelt, the thirty-second and longest-serving president of the United States (1933–1945), was governor of New York in 1932 with aspirations for the presidency. Did you know the following?

* During the 1932 election, FDR portrayed himself as an optimist
* FDR overwhelmed Hoover in the election
* Despite FDR's tone of hope, banks continued to fail and he ordered a "bank holiday"
* He initiated radio addresses to Americans, changing peoples' perception of the presidency

POINTS

TAKING ACTION

Roosevelt believed it was necessary to take action as president to overcome the Depression. Were you aware of the following?

* He cut veterans' pensions and federal employees' salaries
* He pushed for the repeal of Prohibition
* He created employment with massive federal programs
* He created the Tennessee Valley Authority, bringing electricity to the South
* The National Recovery Administration was launched to control business practices

POINTS

SPENDING BIG

Roosevelt pushed ahead with his "New Deal" programs, bringing a new level of government action into American lives. Did you know the following?

* While the NRA was declared unconstitutional, other programs were instituted
* The Civil Works Administration employed 4 million people at the end of 1933
* The Public Works Administration spent billions on public improvement projects
* Despite 20 percent unemployment, midterm elections reinforced FDR's views and policies
* The Works Progress Administration provided work for 3.5 million people

POINTS

COMBINED POINTS

FDR'S LEGACY

In addition to temporary work programs, Roosevelt established some institutions that endure to this day. Which of the following happened during FDR's administration?

A. The Federal Deposit Insurance Corporation was created in 1933 to protect bank deposits
B. The National Labor Relations Act gave protection to unions in 1935
C. Also in 1935, FDR signed the Social Security Act, providing federal assistance to the elderly
D. The nation's first permanent federal income tax was established
E. The Securities and Exchange Commission was created in 1934 to regulate Wall Street

ANSWER: A, B, C, and E

POINTS

MAKING ENEMIES

Roosevelt faced opposition on a political level. Are you aware of these facts?

* The American Liberty League formed, accusing FDR of socialism
* Roosevelt's broad public support allowed him to defeat their challenges
* Roosevelt's greatest antagonist was the Supreme Court
* The court ruled in 1935 that the NRA's regulation of commerce was unconstitutional
* He considered expanding the court to insert friendlier members

POINTS

THE LONG UPHILL

Whether the Depression continued despite of or because of Roosevelt's efforts, Roosevelt was undaunted. Did you know the following?

* Roosevelt won a landslide election in 1936 and saw fit to introduce more drastic measures
* He ordered federal spending cuts, reducing the federal deficit severely
* The meager economic growth came to a halt
* In four months, 2 million people lost their jobs; unemployment hit 20 percent
* To reverse course, in 1938 Roosevelt ordered $3.4 billion in new spending

POINTS

COMBINED POINTS

TROUBLE ON THE HORIZON

New Deal efforts continued, but at a slower pace until the start of World War II. Do you know the following about FDR's actions during this period?

* The Fair Labor Standards Act of 1938 created the minimum wage
* The Act also set the work week at forty hours and prohibited most employment of children
* With unemployment still at seventeen percent, FDR won re-election easily in 1940
* FDR saw opportunities to supply war material to our allies in the Lend-Lease Act
* Soon, U.S. factories were at full capacity and would remain so throughout the war

POINTS

A CHANGE IN THE WHITE HOUSE

Harry S. Truman was our thirty-third president (1945–1953), vice president at the time of Roosevelt's death shortly after the beginning his fourth term. Did you know the following?

* Truman served during World War I as an artillery officer in France
* He was a senator from Missouri who gained prominence fighting waste during WWII
* He had served as vice president for eighty-two days when Roosevelt died
* He became president without much knowledge of world affairs or domestic policies

POINTS

JUST GETTING STARTED

Harry Truman stepped into the role of president in the middle of a world war and he began learning his duties immediately. Were you aware of the following?

* Truman found out about the Manhattan Project on the day of Roosevelt's death
* Victory in Europe was declared four weeks later, on May 8, 1945
* Truman's first decision involved using an atomic bomb on Japan
* Japan rejected the Potsdam Declaration, which called for the country's surrender or utter destruction
* Due to Japan's intransigence, Truman authorized the use of atomic weapons to end the war

POINTS [ ]

COMBINED POINTS [ ]

TIME TO REBUILD

With the war over, Truman faced problems at home and abroad. Did you know the following?

* Conflicts between labor and management, dormant during the war, were renewed
* There were severe shortages in housing and many consumer products
* Sharp increases in demand for goods caused high inflation, hitting six percent per month
* Truman seized control of the railroads after a 1946 strike
* The Truman Doctrine, which called for the containment of Soviet aggression, would become Cold War policy
* The Marshall Plan enabled the rebuilding of war-ravaged Europe

POINTS

WE LIKED IKE

Dwight D. Eisenhower was the thirty-fourth American president (1953–1961) and a five-star general in the U.S. Army. Did you know the following about Eisenhower?

* Eisenhower graduated from West Point in 1915
* He showed extraordinary leadership and diplomatic skills, earning respect from associates
* His abilities were tested in the D-Day landings, and he was not certain they would succeed
* He had prepared a speech taking responsibility for the failure of the operation
* At the end of the war, he helped German citizens receive decent treatment

POINTS

COMBINED POINTS

PEACETIME SERVICE

Like Ulysses Grant, Eisenhower was destined to serve his country in time of peace as well as war. Were you aware of the following?

* In 1948 Eisenhower became president of Columbia University
* He ran for president in 1952, promising to end the Korean War and fight communism
* As president he authorized the creation of the Interstate Highway System in 1956
* The CIA under Eisenhower deposed the leaders of Iran and Guatemala
* In 1957, Eisenhower sent troops to enforce integration in Little Rock, Arkansas
* In his farewell speech, he warned about the influence of the military-industrial complex

POINTS

AMERICAN CAMELOT

John F. Kennedy's service as thirty-fifth president (1961–1963) was brief but eventful. Did you know the following?

* He was a U.S. representative and senator from Massachusetts before running for president
* His debates with Nixon marked the point when television became important in politics
* He is the only president to have won a Pulitzer Prize, for *Profiles in Courage*
* He felt bullied by Nikita Khrushchev during their first meeting in 1961
* While a threat to world peace, the Cuban Missile Crisis improved JFK's approval rating

POINTS

COMBINED POINTS

SCORING YOURSELF: POLITICS

Based on your responses to the checklists in the preceding section, use the rating system below to determine how you stand as an intellectual in the field of politics.

0–12: You lead a very sheltered life.

13–25: You wouldn't be a significant threat on the debating team.

26–38: You have a comfortable knowledge of the political world.

39–49: You are highly attuned to the political sphere.

Chapter 6

The Sciences, Technology, and Mathematics

The checklists covering the Sciences, Technology, and Mathematics are drawn from the physical and natural world and represent some of the facts that the well-rounded intellectual should know.

As you read through the checklists, give yourself one point for correctly identifying all the elements in a checklist or for correctly answering the question posed. At the end of the section you'll have the opportunity to rate how intellectual you are on these subjects.

WHOSE CONTRIBUTION IS THIS

Match the scientist to the contribution.

A. Werner Heisenberg	1. Radioactivity
B. Marie Curie	2. Discovery of the electron
C. Joseph J. Thomson	3. Continental drift
D. Dmitri Mendeleev	4. Periodic table of elements
E. Alfred Wegener	5. Quantum theory

ANSWER: A, 5; B, 1; C, 2; D, 4; E, 3

POINTS

I'LL TAKE ONE

Our early ancestors were more concerned with survival, so mathematics developed slowly. Are you aware of the following facts?

* Early societies used a counting system of "one, two, many"
* Any quantity larger than two was referred to as "many"
* Humans were counting objects 35,000 years ago
* A baboon fibula is the oldest counting artifact

POINTS

WANT TO TRADE

Commerce propelled the use of numbers. Did you know the following?

* Early Middle Eastern traders used small clay shards as counting tokens
* Counting boards superseded the token system
* Counting boards had different sections for 1s, 10s, and 100s
* Sumerians developed the abacus around 2700 B.C.

POINTS

COMBINED POINTS

THE EARLY DAYS

Our knowledge of our place in the universe is constantly increasing. Did you know the following?

* Scientists estimate that the earth is 4.6 billion years old
* The earliest human activity appeared about 2.7 million years ago
* *Homo erectus*, a hominid dating to 1.8 million years ago, migrated to Europe
* *Homo erectus* lived in a number of sites but probably died out
* Neanderthals may have descended from *Homo erectus*

POINTS

MODERNS COME OF AGE

Were you aware of the following facts about our ancestors?

* Our species, *Homo sapiens*, evolved from *Homo erectus*
* This change occurred in Africa about 150,000 years ago
* *Homo sapiens* reached full biological maturity about 50,000 years ago
* These early humans used language and music
* They migrated out of Africa about 70,000 years ago

POINTS

PLACES TO GO

Did you know these facts about early human life?

* Modern humans spread to Eurasia and Oceania by 40,000 years ago
* They reached the Americas by at least 14,500 years ago
* It is believed that they may have coexisted but eventually displaced other species
* Neanderthals became extinct about 30,000 years ago

POINTS

COMBINED POINTS

SETTLING DOWN

Civilization took a while to catch on, but it quickly became popular. Did you know the following?

* Until about 10,000 years ago, most humans were hunter-gatherers
* Small nomadic groups lived without permanent domiciles
* Agriculture, the domestication of animals, and metal tools led to permanent settlements
* This Neolithic Revolution—with food surpluses—encouraged trade and cooperation
* As a result, more complex and larger societies were created

POINTS

HAND ME THAT RULER

A means to measure length and weight was needed for building. How many of these facts were you aware of?

* People have had measuring standards for at least 5,000 years
* Ancient Egyptians measured property after Nile floods
* Pyramid construction required sophisticated calculations
* Egyptians used a decimal, or base 10, system of counting
* Egyptians had symbols for numbers up to one million

POINTS

THERE ARE THREE SIDES
TO EVERY STORY

Pythagoras (ca. 580–500 B.C.) developed the most famous theory in geometry, the Pythagorean theorem. Did you know these other facts about him?

* Pythagoras founded a school of philosophy
* The Pythagoreans believed the physical world was explained by mathematical principles
* Pythagoras showed the mathematical basis for musical pitch and harmony
* Socrates and Plato were influenced by his mathematical world view

POINTS

COMBINED POINTS

EVOLVING IDEAS

Charles Darwin's work on evolution is familiar, but did you know the following facts?

* As a young man, Darwin studied medicine and the ministry
* All 1,250 copies of the first edition *On the Origin of Species* were sold in one day
* From his reading, Darwin acquired the concept of "deep time"
* In *Origin,* Darwin estimated the earth's age at 306 million years

POINTS

A SEA VOYAGE

Darwin's five-year voyage on the *HMS Beagle* was formative, but did you realize the following?

* Darwin was invited to sail on the *HMS Beagle* as company for Captain Robert FitzRoy
* The survey ship's mission was to chart coastal waters for the navy
* Captain FitzRoy hoped to find evidence for the biblical theory of creation
* Darwin and the captain's different viewpoints caused much friction

POINTS

BACK HOME

Darwin did not develop his theories during the voyage of the *Beagle*. Did you know the following?

* This adventure would last him a lifetime—he never left England again
* He acquired specimens and fossils sufficient for his further work
* He discovered a new species of dolphin
* He developed a new theory that coral atolls require a million years to form

POINTS

COMBINED POINTS

THE LONG ROAD TO PUBLICATION

Origin (1859) had a lengthy gestation period. Were you aware of these facts?

* It wasn't until six years after the *Beagle* voyage that Darwin started work on *Origin*
* He worked on his notes for two years and then stopped
* He spent eight years writing a work about barnacles
* *Vestiges of the Natural History of Creation* was published in 1844
* Written anonymously, the book suggest humans were descended from lesser primates

POINTS

COMPETITION

It's possible that Darwin might never have published *Origin*. Did you know the following?

* A young naturalist, Alfred Russel Wallace, contacted Darwin in 1858
* Independently, Wallace had developed a theory of natural selection like Darwin's
* Darwin compromised and they presented a joint summary at the Linnaean Society
* The next year, Darwin published *Origin* and the theory became known as his alone

POINTS

AN UPHILL STRUGGLE

Origin was not greeted with acclaim by the scientific community. Did you know the following?

* Darwin's theory on the process of evolution required more time than the accepted age of the earth allowed
* There was no fossil evidence to support the transitional forms his theory required
* There were many who did not believe that complicated organs developed in stages
* Even Darwin himself thought the idea "absurd"

POINTS

COMBINED POINTS

THE NEXT BIG THING

It wasn't until he published *The Descent of Man* that Darwin expressed his beliefs on human lineage. Are you aware of the following?

* *The Descent of Man, and Selection in Relation to Sex* was published in 1871
* The human/ape lineage theory was not supported by contemporary fossil evidence
* Darwin presented the view that sexual selection was responsible for animal features
* Darwin maintained that despite their differences, all humans are one species

POINTS

A PROLIFIC AUTHOR

Despite deteriorating health, Darwin published many books. Which of the following was not one of Darwin's works?

A. *The Voyage of the Beagle* (1839)
B. *The Expression of the Emotions in Man and Animals* (1872)
C. *The Effects of Cross and Self Fertilization in the Vegetable Kingdom* (1876)
D. *The Formation of Vegetable Mould through the Action of Worms* (1881)
E. *The Consequences of Mollusk Deposition on Hardwood* (1882)

ANSWER: E

POINTS

MISCONCEPTIONS

Did you know these facts about Darwin?

* Evolution as a concept was in use for decades by the time of Darwin
* Darwin theorized how organisms pass along survival advantages
* Darwin did not use the phrase "survival of the fittest"
* He didn't use the term "evolution" until the sixth edition of *Origin*

POINTS

COMBINED POINTS

OF GEEKS AND GREEKS

The ancient Greeks made significant advances in mathematics. Did you know the following?

* The Greeks were using a numbering system, geometry, and proofs by 600 B.C.
* Euclid (ca. 300 B.C.) is known as the father of geometry
* Euclid's *Elements* collected everything known about geometry
* *Elements* was a successful textbook—it was used for 2,000 years

POINTS [   ]

BABBLE ON

The Babylonians (today's Turkey and Syria) were using mathematics 4,500 years ago. Did you know the following?

* Clay tablets were used for calculations
* One cuneiform symbol was used for the number *1* and another for *10*
* The position of digits was significant
* Babylonians used a base-60 system instead of our base-10 system

POINTS [   ]

AND THE GLORY

How many kingdoms are there in the scientific classification system, and do you know them all?

* Plantae
* Animalia
* Fungi
* Protista
* Archaea
* Bacteria

ANSWER: There are six kingdoms

POINTS

COMBINED POINTS

LOOK CLOSELY

What are the differences among these types of mono-cellular animals?

* *Bacteria* are single-celled prokaryotic organisms
* *Archaeans* are similar to bacteria, but they have different genes and enzymes than bacteria
* *Protista* are more like animals, but have characteristics of plants and fungi

POINTS

A SURPRISING FIND

When were microbes first discovered?

Microbes were discovered by Anton van Leeuwenhoek using a microscope of his own design in _____

ANSWER: 1675

POINTS

IT'S ALL RELATIVE

Match these animals with their closest relatives.

A. Manatee

B. Tapir

C. Panda bear

1. Raccoons

2. Elephants

3. Horses and rhinoceroses

ANSWER: A, 2; B, 3; C, 1

POINTS

COMBINED POINTS

A BETTER WAY OF THINKING

British geologist Charles Lyell (1797–1875) had a profound influence on Darwin. Did you know this about him?

* Some geologists of his time believed the Earth was shaped by cataclysmic events
* Catastrophism allowed for biblical happenings like Noah's flood
* Lyell was a uniformitarianist
* Uniformitarianism held that the Earth changed slowly over long spans of time

POINTS

NOT PERFECT

Lyell and the uniformitarians, despite the soundness of their ideas, were incorrect about many geological concepts. Were you aware of the following?

* Lyell did not think that glaciers were responsible for change
* Lyell refused to accept the idea of ice ages
* He believed that animals had existed relatively unchanged since the beginning of time
* He did not believe that animal species could become extinct

POINTS

THE BASICS

Despite his scientific shortsightedness on some topics, Lyell's work was important to Darwin. Did you know the following?

* Lyell first published his *Principles of Geology* in 1830
* Darwin had a first edition of *Principles* with him on the *Beagle* voyage
* The book, which saw twelve editions printed, influenced geologic thinking for a century
* Not until the tenth edition of *Principles* did Lyell endorse evolution

POINTS

COMBINED POINTS

WHO'S WHO

Can you match the famous mathematician with his contribution?

1. Al-Khwarizmi		A. Wrote *Conics*
2. Apollonius		B. Wrote *Arithmetica*
3. Descartes		C. Developed algebra
4. Diophantus		D. Founded spherical trigonometry
5. Menelaus		E. Founded analytic geometry

ANSWER: 1, C; 2, A; 3, E; 4, B; 5, D

POINTS

OFF BASE

Different counting systems, other than our base-10 system, have influenced us to this day. Did you know the following?

* The base-60 system is why we have 60 seconds in a minute and 60 minutes in an hour
* The base-20 system is heard in French numbers: *quatre-vingt* means "four-twenty"
* The base-20 system was found in the former British monetary system
* The base-12 system can be found in our measurement of hours in a day and months in a year

POINTS

TRULY NOBLE

What are the noble gases?

* Helium
* Neon
* Argon
* Krypton
* Xenon
* Radon

HOW ABOUT STATE OF MIND

Can you name the states of matter?

* Gas
* Liquid
* Solid
* Plasma

POINTS

WHEN WAS THAT

In which year was the transistor invented?

A. 1940
B. 1956
C. 1962
D. 1984

ANSWER: B, 1956, by John Bardeen

POINTS

A VISIONARY

The history of computers dates, improbably, to the nineteenth century. Are you acquainted with the following facts?

* English mathematician Charles Babbage (1791–1871) is considered "father of the computer"
* Babbage conceived of a machine to reduce errors in contemporary calculations
* He started work on a prototype "difference engine" in the 1820s
* He received ample funding but completed only a fragment of the project
* The steam-powered machine would have weighed 15 tons and required 25,000 parts
* A working model of his updated design was built in 1990

POINTS

COMBINED POINTS

AN ENGINEERING PROBLEM

Babbage was undaunted despite his inability to complete the difference engine. Did you know the following about his later efforts?

* Babbage started work on a more complex machine called an "analytical engine"
* The analytical engine was not a single machine but a series of designs
* It could be programmed using punched cards—a technique used until the 1970s
* Ada Lovelace (1815–1852) wrote the first computer program for the machine
* The analytical engine could operate on numbers with up to fifty decimal places

POINTS

A HOT TOPIC

Other scientists were working in the field of computing in the late 1800s. Did you know the following?

* American scientist Herman Hollerith built the first electromechanical "tabulator"
* The machine was put to use by the U.S. Census Bureau in 1890
* The success of his design inspired him to form the Tabulating Machine Company in 1896
* By 1924, the company was called International Business Machines (IBM)

POINTS

EUROPEAN DEVELOPMENTS

Are you aware of early computer developments in Germany?

* In 1936, German scientist Konrad Zuse built the first programmable binary computer
* Notably, he adopted the binary system of converting numbers to zeroes and ones
* This system is also called "digital computing"
* His machine was controlled by perforated strips of discarded movie film
* The machine was destroyed in an air raid on Berlin in 1943

POINTS

COMBINED POINTS

ANOTHER QUIP

The Incas had no written language and a huge empire to administer. Did you know the following?

* A quipo was a cord of cotton with additional knotted cords attached
* The quipo was used to record and transmit information
* The number of knots, their position, size, and color were significant
* A quipo with 1,800 cords has been discovered

POINTS

QUOTABLE

Who is quoted as saying about Sir Isaac Newton: "Nature to him was an open book, whose letters he could read without effort?"

1. Bertrand Russell
2. Stephen Hawking
3. Albert Einstein
4. J. Robert Oppenheimer

ANSWER: 3

POINTS

SIR ISAAC

Sir Isaac Newton left an indelible impression on the fields of science and mathematics. Were you aware of the following?

* He built the first practical reflecting telescope
* His *Principia* (1687) is among the most influential books in the history of science
* The *Principia* explains the behavior of celestial bodies and the law of gravitation
* He competes with Gottfried Wilhelm Leibniz for credit of having developed infinitesimal calculus

POINTS

COMBINED POINTS

TURING'S WORK

How many of the following facts about English mathematician Alan Turing are you familiar with?

* Turing (1912–1954) published a computer theory in 1937
* His paper can be considered as the foundation of computer science
* He formalized the concepts of algorithm and computation
* During World War II, he worked for Britain's code-breaking center on German ciphers
* His techniques were fundamental in breaking the German Enigma codes

POINTS

WAR EFFORTS

Codebreaking was critical to the Allied war efforts in the 1940s. Are you aware of the following?

* English engineer Thomas Flowers also worked on the British code-breaking efforts
* In 1943 he built Colossus, the world's first programmable digital electronic computer
* Ten Colossus machines were built to perform the data crunching decryption duties
* All the computers were destroyed in 1945 to maintain secrecy
* Their existence only became generally known in the 1970s

POINTS

ADDING IT ALL UP

Military requirements prompted the creation of another historical technological development. Are you familiar with these facts?

* The Electronic Numerical Integrator and Computer was contracted by the Army in 1943
* ENIAC was designed to compute firing and bombing tables for the military
* It went into use in 1946 and was in continuous operation until 1955
* ENIAC consisted of thirty units, had 18,000 vacuum tubes, and weighed thirty tons
* It was used later to make calculations used in designing the hydrogen bomb

POINTS

COMBINED POINTS

ADDING TO THE BOTTOM LINE

It took further developments before the use of computers could expand.
Were you aware of the following?

* The transistor was invented in 1947 at AT&T Bell Labs
* Replacing vacuum tubes with transistors made computers faster and
  smaller
* IBM became the primary supplier of mainframe computers to
  business
* From the 1960s on, mainframes took over the processing of computing tasks

POINTS

MUCH ADO

A famous problem in mathematics, finally solved in 1995, was Fermat's Last Theorem. Do you know these facts:

* The theorem: $x^n + y^n = z^n$ has no integer solutions for $n > 2$ and x, y, and z are positive
* Fermat first proposed this problem in 1637
* He wrote the problem in the margin of his *Arithmetica*
* He claimed he had a proof, but it wouldn't fit
* Countless mathematicians attempted to solve the problem for 358 years

POINTS [   ]

HE SHOULD KNOW

According to Johannes Kepler, what are the two "treasures of geometry"?

* The Pythagorean theorem ($a^2 + b^2 = c^2$)
* The golden ratio ($a+b/b = a/b \equiv \varphi$)

POINTS [   ]

COMBINED POINTS [   ]

LANDMARKS IN MATHEMATICS

Match the mathematicians with their works:

A. Descartes

B. Fibonacci

C. Plato

D. Kepler

1. *Harmonices Mundi*

2. *La Géométrie*

3. *Liber Abaci*

4. *Timaeus*

ANSWER: A, 2; B, 3; C, 4; D,1

POINTS

THE BETTER PART OF VALOR

Discrete mathematics studies noncontinuous events. Can you name four areas of discrete mathematics?

* Computing—the binary language of computers is discrete
* Probability—from the simple coin toss to meteorology
* Graph theory—examines networks and paths
* Logic—the study of true/false relationships

POINTS

IT'S OBVIOUS

What is the difference between a eukaryote and a prokaryote?

* Eukaryotes have a defined nucleus and as well as other organelles
  such as Golgi apparatus
* Prokaryotes are cells without a nucleus or other organelles
* Prokaryotes don't have internal membranes

POINTS

COMBINED POINTS

AT THE BEGINNING

Where can you find one of the earliest forms of life?

* In the Marble Bar area of Australia
* Fossilized remains of cyanobacteria called stromatolites are more than 3 billion years old
* Their living descendents are estimated to be several thousand years old
* They can be found in the Hamelin Pool Marine Nature Reserve in the Sharks Bay area of Australia

POINTS

ISLAND LIFE

Which of these are not volcanic islands?

A. The Hawaiian Islands
B. Line Islands
C. Lesser Antilles
D. Madagascar

ANSWER: D

POINTS

STAND BACK

Which of these volcanoes is not active?

A. Mount Vesuvius
B. Mount Kilauea
C. Mount St. Helens
D. The Hohentwiel

ANSWER: D

POINTS

COMBINED POINTS

IN THE BEGINNING

The ubiquitous Internet, like many good ideas, had humble origins. Did you know the following?

* The Internet's first incarnation was called ARPANET
* The U.S. Department of Defense proposed the ARPANET research project in 1967
* The project was designed to facilitate communication between two computers
* UCLA and Stanford were the two nodes of this network, which went live in 1969
* E-mail was added in 1972 and quickly became its main service

POINTS

NOW YOU SEE IT . . .

Can you name the eight different electromagnetic spectrums?

* Radio
* Microwave
* Infrared
* Visible
* Ultraviolet
* X-rays
* Gamma rays
* High energy gamma rays

POINTS

WAVES OF MANY LENGTHS

What are the different types of wavelength?

* Microwave
* Shortwave
* Medium wave
* Long wave

POINTS

COMBINED POINTS

LOOKS WINDY

Did you know these facts about El Niño and La Niña?

* El Nino/La Nina are part of a weather pattern
* This weather pattern occurs in the Pacific Ocean roughly every 4–5 years
* It is characterized by a warming or cooling of the surface ocean temperature
* El Niño happens when the ocean gets warmer
* La Niña occurs when the ocean gets cooler

POINTS

WE'RE NOT ALONE

What is the most numerous type of animal on Earth?

A. Insects
B. Mites
C. Nematodes

ANSWER: C

POINTS

WISH YOU WERE HERE

How many of these natural oddities have you seen?

* La Brea Tar Pits
* The Great Salt Lake
* The Dead Sea

POINTS

COMBINED POINTS

SCORING YOURSELF: SCIENCE, TECHNOLOGY, AND MATHEMATICS

Based on your responses to the checklists in the preceding section, use the rating system below to determine how you stand as an intellectual in science, technology, and mathematics.

0–11: A scientist may have frightened you at a young age.

12–28: You probably struggled with the sciences in school.

29–43: Your scientific knowledge should enable you to read and understand many technical articles.

44–60: At MIT they speak of you in hushed tones.

Conclusion

If you've read all the checklists in this book, then you've been exposed to a highly diverse collection of topics and facts. These checklists were designed to test the depth and breadth of your intellect, expose your tastes and preferences, and give you the opportunity to demonstrate your interests and pastimes.

Undoubtedly some readers will feel that these checklists do not fairly represent a subject area. Admittedly, space limitations prevented a balanced approach to the topics covered. If you are expert in fields or themes not covered, congratulations on your achievements. If the checklists in this book have played to your strengths, you too deserve congratulations for your knowledge.

THE FINAL SCORE SHEET

After you have scored all the sections in *The Intellectual's Checklist*, you can use the final rating device to determine your overall standing as an intellectual. Add up the individual scores you recorded for the ratings at the end of each section, then see where your total occurs in the scale below.

0–85: Clearly, you need to study more.

91–176: A respectable showing, but you have too few laurels to consider resting.

182–267: You qualify for recognition by your peers.

293–357: You have reason to be proud.

Index